What people are saying about

Lessons I Have Unlearned

Florence makes you feel like you are having a heart to heart with an old friend. She is honest about the reality of life and vulnerable about her own journey in a way that is refreshing and screams 'you are not alone!'. Florence wades right in to discussions about identity and spirituality, speaking to those inner voices which all of us battle, with clarity and fluency. I highly recommend this book for every person, because we all battle fear and insecurity and have to come to terms with a life which has not turned out the way we expected. There are no easy answers, but this book is an encouragement that hope remains.
Selina Stone, Tutor and Lecturer in Political Theology at St Mellitus College

Witty and cutthroat, Florence managed to shred me to pieces whilst I laughed out loud in public. An insightful exploration of the madness of postmodern life, calling us back to a truth we all once knew: that intimacy with God and each other can never be replaced.
Tom Cozens, Director of owlinspace

This book is a wonderful testament to Gildea's splendid intellect and humanity. It is a deeply moving and personal description of the fight against mental illness and the role that faith can play in coming out the other side.
Frank Field, Member of Parliament 1979–2019

Very few books meet you where you're at, making no assumptions about you and gently ease you into the absolute common sense of believing and saying yes to Jesus and his Kingdom. This one does.

Martin Saunders, Deputy CEO of Youthscape and author of *The Man You're Made To Be*

This is a gem of a book, packed with biblical wisdom, honesty and hope. It blessed me and will help many others.

Emma Scrivener, Author of *A New Name: Grace and Healing for Anorexia; A New Day: Moving on from Hunger, Anxiety, Control, Shame, Anger and Despair,* and *What Does the Bible Really Say About Eating Disorders?*

This book is a rich, wise and thoughtful exploration of some of the deepest issues facing young adults today. Read it to be challenged, informed and inspired.

Reverend Mark Woods, Editor at the Bible Society, Baptist Minister. And author of *Does the Bible Really Say That? Challenging our Assumptions in the Light of Scripture.*

Lessons I Have Unlearned

Because Life Doesn't Look Like It Did in the Pictures

Lessons I Have Unlearned

Because Life Doesn't Look Like It Did in the Pictures

Florence Gildea

CIRCLE
BOOKS

Winchester, UK
Washington, USA

JOHN HUNT PUBLISHING

First published by Circle Books, 2021
Circle Books is an imprint of John Hunt Publishing Ltd., No. 3 East St., Alresford,
Hampshire SO24 9EE, UK
office@jhpbooks.com
www.johnhuntpublishing.com
www.circle-books.com

For distributor details and how to order please visit the 'Ordering' section on our website.

Text copyright: Florence Gildea 2020

ISBN: 978 1 78904 575 8
978 1 78904 576 5 (ebook)
Library of Congress Control Number: 2020930846

A CIP catalogue record for this book is available from the British Library.

Design: Stuart Davies

UK: Printed and bound by CPI Group (UK) Ltd, Croydon, CR0 4YY
Printed in North America by CPI GPS partners

We operate a distinctive and ethical publishing philosophy in
all areas of our business, from our global network of authors to
production and worldwide distribution.

Contents

For my mum, for everything.

Acknowledgments

I never thought I had a book in me until Caroline Heath-Taylor told me I did, and I would have likely deleted the manuscript without the cheerleading of Katherine Haylett. But I am indebted also to every one of my friends who has opened up to me and helped me to realise that maybe it wasn't just me who was learning to mind the gap between our expectations and reality.

Introduction

I didn't expect my life to look like this.

These words have come out of my own mouth more times than I can count. They've been uttered too by my friends on park benches and pews, in coffee shops and public bathrooms, over the phone and through a screen as, one by one, their hearts have been broken by the harsh realities of growing up. These words have come out in forced laughs, in gasps between tears, and in pained sighs. I feel like I know them inside and out, back to front, like they're etched somewhere deep inside my soul.

We grew up with the expectation that life would be easy, that there was a conveyor belt which we could jump on and be carried through from one milestone to the next. Go to university, get on the career ladder, then the property ladder, fall in love, get married, have a family. Then, sit back, relax and enjoy. We also knew exactly who we wanted to be when we grew up. I eagerly looked forward for the day when she'd be there staring back at me in the mirror: the woman-who-had-it-all. Confident and bubbly, smart and beautiful; a go-getter who was also the life and soul of the party. This was the ideal, the type of person destined for stardom and success. And, in a culture cluttered with rags-to-riches stories and reality TV contests, we didn't want to be a statistic: we wanted to be a somebody.

Maybe it's a sign of how fortunate we were growing up that we made these assumptions. For some people, from the moment they open their eyes, the world strikes them as cruel. But recognising that seems to offer little comfort when your expectations are shattered and you're left wondering why you have forfeited the smooth journey through life that you thought was your due, and whether it was because you did something wrong. Often, looking for an easy target, we heap blame on ourselves for taking a wrong turn, rather than reckoning that joy and heartache are hopelessly entangled, and that no life, not even a single chapter of it, is free from challenge or pain. Nope, we cross our arms, stick our chins forward and stubbornly insist that it must be possible to lead a life reminiscent of a feel-good movie; it's just that we've slipped up somewhere. The conveyor belt really does exist, we just need to find our way back onto it.

But then it happens again. And again. And either we are left feeling like we are hopelessly broken and incapable of being in the world, or the penny drops: life isn't like the movies. It will never look like it did in the pictures.

I grew up with a clear road map for my life, and enough gumption to think I could bring it into reality. It wasn't so much one I designed for myself as one I absorbed by osmosis. My parents went to Cambridge University, so I planned to go there as well. My mum was a successful career woman, so I aimed to boast of power suits and a six-figure salary. A husband and 2.4 children seemed an inevitable part of the package deal. This was the only way I could envision success, and my school reports were positive enough for me to presume that was within reach. All I had to do, I thought, was try hard and keep to the rules. Then everything would go as planned.

But it didn't. Before I had even left home, that blueprint was torn into shreds. By the time I was seventeen, battling mental illness, feelings of self-loathing and inadequacy had become my full-time job, my every breath. The world I had thought was so easily controllable came to seem unfathomably chaotic and unkind. Even the person I thought I was – vivacious, outgoing and confident – had been lost beneath the waves. Life has never since felt like a train-track. It's more like an etch-a-sketch: random, circuitous, and sometimes I lose sight of the line altogether.

And yet, that random squiggle is more beautiful than any neat flowchart I could have designed for myself. Because God has peppered that path with love and beauty and joy in the most unexpected places. It was at rock bottom that I first properly encountered Jesus as someone more than a baby in a manger or an animated figure in a cartoon from Religious Education lessons. It was in a dark, dank pit of despair that I heard of this thing called grace and its promise that there was nothing I could do to make God love me more or less. I grabbed onto it with all the faith I could muster. Postage stamp-sized as it was, it was enough to keep me going. I would have liked a battleship kind of rescue – one which meant I could plough through the waves and never again be jolted or jostled from my course. But it was more like a makeshift life raft: something to hold onto, something to save me from myself, but which I could not steer or direct. It would have to be God who captained the vessel. I would be saved by grace and live by grace, dependent on it each day.

Continuing to take life one step at a time, I have no route mapped out for myself let alone anyone else. But there's something about sharing stories – a secret, gentle power which strengthens our souls. When we first find ourselves at ground zero, we scramble about for anything to start building with so that we don't have to fully reckon with our feelings of hurt and betrayal. We cry out to God for a plan to tell us what to build and to give us the tools to help us do it as quickly as possible – ideally before anyone notices that we are falling apart at the seams. In my experience, God often tries something else: He draws out other dwellers in the wilderness. We didn't notice them at first because we instinctively jumped into self-protection mode, but there they are, emerging from the shadows, bearing wounds which resemble ours. He doesn't plaster over the pain, but He somehow makes us whole, by binding us to the similarly wounded. Although the life we were building for ourselves remains debris at our feet, travelling with these fellow nomads gives us an undeniable sense of home.

We didn't think we'd end up here. This isn't the one we circled in the catalogue. But God has already trod this ground before you. And trust me, even here, off the map, is holy ground.

Some books give you diagnostic labels to attach to yourself after a dose of rumination and self-introspection – a number or a series of letters that are apparently the key to unlocking who you are and how you came to be so. I've turned to them in the past to try to work out what setting I am stuck on. They can be helpful, but these labels can also be too sticky for their own good – other weapons to hit ourselves over the head with; identities that feel like prisons; other phrases we use as synonyms for 'not good enough' or 'not who I wish I was'. I haven't the expertise to so specifically categorise the cause of your woes. But I know one thing you are, one of the most important things about you actually, and that is that you are not alone. I know that you never have been and you never will be.

I think you need to know that more than you need another cliched fridge magnet telling you to make lemonade with the lemons life has given you, or that every cloud has a silver lining. The positive affirmations that circulate endlessly on social media long ago began to sound vapid. The truth is you deserve better. You have come to a place where complexity and nuance abound, and there can be no squeezing life back into neat compartments and categories. Debris can never again be a puzzle piece. But there is freedom in unpicking the lies that got under our skin and chipped away at our joy. The ones we absorbed and amen'd because we were so eager to please and so desperate to fit in. These are the lessons I have unlearned so far, and the ones I imagine you're peeling back too.

1. How to have everything under control

Supreme above our cravings for caffeine, crisps and chocolate is our addiction to control. Since the dawn of time, we've sought to satiate our longing for peace, contentment and security through owning and controlling what we can. From the first bite of the forbidden fruit, we have wanted God-like mastery over the world around us. Sometimes we've used spiritual means to tell us the future and shape it to our liking, as with the ancient practices of divination, sorcery and superstition. But now we mostly succour our addiction with technology – it gives us say over the shape of our bodies through plastic surgery, over the DNA of potentially any living organism through genetic engineering, and, with virtual reality, can even allow us to create whole new worlds, just the way we want them. And if the independence of other people irritates your need for control, then you can always surround yourself with companion robots, virtual assistants, dating simulations and avatars – programmed to heed your every command, answer your every query, and all without the risk of conflict or desertion.

The unknowable, the unpredictable, the unfathomable are all shrinking domains, crowded out by projections and strategies, forecasts and filters. Or, at least, we hope they are. Otherwise, we'd have to face the fallibility and frailty of the human condition. We'd have to forego our certainty and to answer questions with 'I don't know'. We'd have to accept our place on earth, often shrouded in fog, rather than aloof above it.

That impulse to minimise uncertainty runs deep within my own heart. In primary school, we were asked whether we'd most like a jet-pack so we could fly or special X-ray glasses which would allow us to read minds. I picked the specs in a heartbeat, and my fantasy of having constant, real-time feedback about what people were thinking about me only grew more intoxicating over time. If I had that, I'd be effectively immune from shame and rejection, which by my late teenage years, I had experienced enough to last a lifetime. Enough to convince me that there was something rotten at my core. Something that, as soon as anyone got close to me, acted like a reverse magnet, propelling them away. I wasn't sure what it was. I couldn't tell if I was too much, not enough, or somehow, paradoxically, both. The not-knowing made it even harder to accept.

I hadn't always felt so toxic. When I was younger, I had a near magical ability with my petite frame, my rosy cheeks and my bookishness to wrap grown-ups around my little finger. But when I went to secondary school, I hit a roadblock. Someone had rudely moved the goalposts without notifying me. If smarts and studiousness had hitherto served me well, they were now my downfall. Instead, well-applied make-up, an apathetic demeanour and popularity with boys were the keys to the top of the social ladder. I, unfortunately, was small, stumpy, with limp, unstyled hair. Evidently, I had peaked too soon.

So, I rearranged the furniture of my personality in an effort to protect myself, hiding the pieces I thought were repellent and adopting whichever traits seemed to earn others' affirmation. I became like a Rubik's cube, twisting to suit every palette, to ensure maximum appeal and minimum conflict. But with each turn, the creak was a little louder, the rub a little more painful: it was obvious that I was playing a part and so I never ended up feeling like I belonged. I was always the one having to prove myself. The butt of the joke. The more people noticed my thin skin, the more they jabbed and prodded at it.

Tired of being exposed as a fraud and left behind, I wanted as much distance as possible from all the selves I had tried to be. There was one makeover left to try. One part of my personality that had been a constant which I could shed, to see if that was what had been the deal-breaker all along: my appetite. I was known for being unreserved around food: a whole loaf of bread for lunch, a family-sized chocolate bar after school, and ordering whatever came with chips and gravy when we went out to eat. I didn't think twice about it. Until now.

How could I have missed it? Every movie and magazine I had ever seen had been quite clear about what a woman had to be in order to be loved: skinny. I had naïvely believed my mum when she told me I was beautiful. From now on, I wouldn't be so cavalier. I would think not just twice but two hundred times about each and every bite. I would submit to what I euphemistically called 'the routine': a meticulous, to-the-minute schedule which governed my every move and my every thought.

First thing before school was porridge – thirty-five grams of oats, ninety millilitres of soya milk, ninety millilitres of water. I added water because even zero-fat, plant-based milk seemed too gluttonous. By eleven in the morning, I'd be near-to-fainting ravenous, counting down the minutes until quarter past twelve when lunchtime began. I would fast lose the ability to concentrate on the work in front of me, but knew I could catch up when I got home since I had done a decent job of pushing my friends away, leaving me with all my evenings and weekends free.

Then lunchtime. I'd punish myself by not opening my lunchbox until fifteen minutes after the bell had gone to delay the next hunger pangs until later in the afternoon, and to prove to myself that I was iron-willed enough to overcome biology, strong enough to last through the light-headedness. Inside my Tupperware was the same lunch I precisely weighed and cooked every night: eight prawns, seven broccoli and cauliflower florets, three baby carrots and thirty-five grams of fresh egg noodles (more expensive but fewer calories than the dried alternative, and it was clear which was my priority). I'd eat the vegetables first, then the prawns and finally the noodles as they did the most to keep me full, and I thought that the three minutes which separated them from the broccoli was crucial to avoid collapsing before the bell went at quarter past three.

After school, I would get off the bus a couple of stops early so I'd have to walk longer and then I'd try to take my mind off the hunger that was building up by doing Pilates with a home exercise video. The video was divided into six five-minute sessions, and I'd aim to do at least three, maximising the amount of work done in each one by beginning each exercise – which I knew off by heart – before the instructor began speaking. The extra 10 seconds or so was bound to burn away more of the body I had come to despise.

The next thing on the bare-bones menu I had drawn up for myself was a hot chocolate (made with water, of course, instead of milk). This was my moment of indulgence: I would watch it in front of the TV (which I gave myself permission to watch for twenty minutes per day) and drink it with a teaspoon so that I could savour every drop. In fact, I ate all meals with a particular teaspoon, mug and bowl which I refused to let anyone else touch, even to wash them. I never ate anything on a plate – a plate seemed too large, too empty, visually demanding to be filled while everything in me cried out to be kept empty.

As the months wore on, my tummy stopped rumbling; it somehow knew that audibly demanding attention was useless. My body didn't make a sound to register its hunger: I simply became unable to move. I would freeze, feeling like a ghost, a hair's width away from oblivion. That was when I knew I had to eat. Only then would I cave. That weakness came each day before it was time to make dinner. I would have a bath beforehand, first, to save energy (fun fact: you can't collapse if you're already lying down) and second, to purify myself before eating. Because the weird thing was that I saw food both as a necessary evil, my need for it serving to trick and torment me, and as a privilege which I didn't deserve in the slightest.

Dinner was always a Weight Watchers' soup, selected on the basis it weighed only three hundred grams rather than the standard four-hundred-gram tin. If I thought about eating a full-sized portion, I could practically feel my cheeks fill and my tummy inflate. Atop the soup I would add a few baby carrots, peas and broccoli florets to persuade my mum that this was a proper meal, just like anyone else would eat. To maintain the facade of normalcy, I'd tear the labels off the soup tins so she wouldn't know they were anything to do with dieting, and prepare all my meals alone. If my mum did walk into the kitchen, I'd drop everything until she left again. My anxiety was so palpable, so visceral, that it didn't take long before she'd retreat. Then, after eating, I would scrub everything to within an inch of its life to burn as many of the freshly consumed calories as possible. I would collapse into bed as early as possible, praying the hunger pangs wouldn't wake me. I kept an oatcake on my bedside table just in case they did. But I knew I wouldn't forgive myself if I succumbed and ate it. Forty-five calories, I'd remind myself to warn myself away from such a midnight feast.

This was my life. This was all of my life. From the moment my eyes opened in the morning to when they buckled under their own weight at night, and every millisecond in between. Any slight adjustment or addition to 'the routine' was unfathomable. If anything came between me and maximum control over the energy I consumed and expended, I would be thrown into a fit of anxiety, lashing my bony arms out at the world which, in that instant, seemed to disdain me more than I loathed myself. If my porridge spilled over in the microwave, I would scream 'why do you hate me?' until my lungs burned. When a shop ran out of one of the few ingredients that I counted 'safe', I would be inconsolable. Everything existed on a knife-edge.

When you're living in cut-throat legalism, with your sights set on absolute perfection, then every moment feels like playing with fire. The stakes are Everest high. Rather than making me feel more secure and contented, I had never been so suffocated with anxiety. I feared my kitchen scales breaking and accidentally eating a few grams more of food than I had prescribed myself.

I was terrified of visitors eating any of my food. And there was always the lurking terror of being caught: of people realising that this was more than a diet, that it was self-destruction. Seeking absolute control wasn't protecting me from loss; it was making it inevitable as not only did my body start to shut down but the spark in me was fading fast. I never laughed anymore; I never even cried.

I didn't even so much as blink when I was warned that, if I kept going as I was, I had maybe a fortnight left. If that prognosis was a scare tactic, it didn't work. If anything, I saw it as an accolade. All I felt was numb. Numb to everything, that is, except the cold. As I walked back to school from that appointment, my stick legs gave out beneath me and I fell, famished, in the snow. I just lay there while *Skinny Love* by Bon Iver played on my MP3 player. 'Come on skinny love, just last the year', he sang over and over while I summoned up the strength to get back on my feet.

This unwitting serenade was pleading with me to stay in the game for at least the four final weeks of December. That meant it was pleading with me to change. I had no desire to do so for my own sake, but nor did I want to break my family's heart. I had thought skinniness led to love; now I knew I was going to have to choose between them. I scrambled back up and staggered drunkenly the rest of the way, woozy with weakness (there was, after all, no way I'd sample even a drop of alcohol – 'empty calories' I used to say self-righteously to myself whenever I saw people drink).

Seven months later, a book arrived from a family friend from way back when. He didn't know that I had become a shell of the girl he had seen grow up. But I presume he thought that my eighteenth birthday was a milestone which might prompt me to have questions about the meaning of life. So he sent me *What's So Amazing About Grace* by Philip Yancey, and my heart did a somersault. 'There's nothing you can do to make God love you more, and there's nothing you can do to make Him love you less', I read. No matter what I eat? No matter what I weigh? No matter how far down the path of self-sabotage I've gone?

I knew barely anything else about Christianity but that was enough to bring me back from the brink. There was no overnight healing. No dramatic before and after. But slowly, slowly, through what I can only describe as imperceptible moves of the Spirit, I was weaned off 'the routine'.

But, the problem with the fact that our experience of God is mediated through our own psyche is that it's very easy to attribute to Him our own hang-ups, preferences and prejudices, to create God in our own image and effectively script His lines with our own thoughts. And I hadn't yet relinquished my presumption that safety came through some form of control, even if it was no longer over food. Nor had I come to accept myself just as I was. So, the scorn and shaming which had previously come from the voice of anorexia, I now unconsciously assigned to God.

The idea of grace kept slipping through my fingers as, whenever I heard about God as an all-powerful, all-seeing judge, He became, in my mind, another person I daren't be vulnerable around, from whom I had to withhold trust in case He suddenly turned on me. I figured that to protect myself, I needed to work to keep God on side. I essentially had to manipulate Him. So, I endeavoured to conform to the rules which would ensure He would rain down blessings rather than wrath. Turn up at church as often as possible – ideally two services a Sunday and one mid-week Bible study. Pay special attention to the sermons to get a head full of right answers and make up for the lack of Christian youth groups and holidays everyone else seemed to have been enjoying while I had been creating my own personal hell. Evangelise my friends at every opportunity. I took my cues from those who were most zealous about their faith – I tried to think like them, speak like them, and act like them. I learned to avoid swearing and flirting and movies rated 15 plus. I thought if I became the ideal Christian, then I would be guaranteed a life free from suffering.

As naïve as it sounds, I'm not the first to assume we can pull God's strings this way. Just flip to the book of Job. Job is one of three books in the Old Testament classified as Wisdom literature, and they can basically be read as a theological tug of war, all wrestling with the question of why suffering happens. The first, Proverbs, argues that there is an order inherent in the world as God designed it, which means that the wise prosper and the foolish flounder. All you have to do to attain the good life and avoid disaster is imbibe and live by its prudent sayings. Simple, and just as I suspected.

But then the second book of Wisdom, Ecclesiastes, brings up the elephant in the room: life is a whole lot messier than that equation implies. It doesn't take too long to realise that bad things happen to good people and to see rewards piling up on the plates of those who have behaved thoughtlessly, selfishly or maliciously. As the preacher of Ecclesiastes remarks: 'I saw that under the sun the race is not to the swift, nor the battle to the strong, nor bread to the wise, nor riches to the intelligent, nor favour to those with knowledge, but time and chance happen to them all' (Ecclesiastes 9:11). This thing called 'chance' messes up any neat order of cause and effect. Everything in life, he says, is 'hevel', a Hebrew word often translated as vanity but which can also be read as 'vapour', 'smoke' or 'mere breath'. There's no solidity to it; it is hard to grapple with, mysterious in the form it takes and the way it moves. Sure, it's best to live wisely, the preacher concludes, but don't think that by that you can avoid the inevitable race of time, evade your own mortality, or control the script of your life.

Yeah, thanks for that one, mate.

That leaves the book of Job, the stage on which these competing views about the good life are played out. Satan believes in a straightforward system of cause and effect: he thinks that people only worship God because it is in their self-interest – being faithful earns them blessings; piety is just a way of getting what they want. So when God tells Satan about how righteous and upright Job is, Satan sneers:

> Does Job fear God for nothing? … Have you not put a hedge around him and his household and everything he has? You have blessed the work of his hands, so that his flocks and herds are spread throughout the land. But now stretch out your hand and strike everything he has, and he will surely curse you to your face. (Job 1:9–11)

In other words, 'of course Job is your biggest fan: you've given him everything he could ever want. But if you took all that away, he'd want nothing to do with you'. So, to prove Satan wrong, God lets disaster strike Job – he loses his children, his good health and his livelihood. And onto the scene enter more characters who believe that there's a contractual logic which undergirds all of life. According to Job's wife and friends, God wields both a carrot and a stick: whether He blesses or punishes is decided by human action. Good behaviour leads to reward and sin leads to punishment. So, the logic runs, for such suffering to afflict Job, Job must have sinned. All he needs to do is repent of what he's done and start to behave more virtuously. Then, everything can go back to normal.

Such myths are powerful, pervasive and attractive because they make us feel safe. You can find modern, secular equivalents everywhere: you only get lung cancer if you smoke; you only become homeless if you don't work hard enough; a husband will only cheat if his wife whines and nags and doesn't keep herself 'in shape'; sexual assaults only happen to those who dressed like they were 'asking for it'. So, to get, and keep hold of, your comfy middle-class lifestyle, all you have to do is work hard, act responsibly, and don't be too demanding. We tell ourselves such tales because it numbs the sense of the unfathomability and unpredictability of life as it actually is – of life as it always is, no matter how well we stick to the rules.

As readers of Job's story, we have insight that none of the characters do: that Job's hardships are paradoxically related to his righteousness. Satan is using him as the perfect test case *because of* his devotion to God. Satan thinks that if he can bring down this epitome of the worshipful servant, then God's whole mission can be undermined. The story brings to life something we all observe sooner or later: tragedy can strike the people who least deserve it. When God finally speaks up at the end of the book, it's clear that Satan and Job's friends have wildly misunderstood how God works.

'Great', I think, as soon as God's voice reappears in the text, 'now to find out how the world really works and how I can make sure I never go through even a fraction of what Job did'. I whip out my notebook only to have my need for control deeply disappointed. God doesn't give a neat exposition on the whys and wherefores of suffering. There's no behind-the-scenes tour of the heavenly showdown between God and Satan. There are no justifications, no apologies, no roadmaps for a pain-free life.

Instead, God switches the lens. He zooms out – far away from the particularities of Job's life, back to the moment of creation.

Where were you when I laid the earth's foundation?
Tell me, if you understand...
Have you ever given orders to the morning,
or shown the dawn its place,
that it might take the earth by the edges
and shake the wicked out of it?...
Can you raise your voice to the clouds
and cover yourself with a flood of water?
Do you send the lightning bolts on their way?...
Do you give the horse its strength
or clothe its neck with a flowing mane?...

Does the eagle soar at your command
and build its nest on high?
(Job 38:4, 12–13, 34 – 35; 39:19, 27)

With every line, I can feel myself shrink. The sense of my own significance crumbles. My perception that life is something for which I can formulate strategies shatters. Time and space – dimensions that previously felt manageable as long as I had Google Maps, measurable in seconds and minutes, metres and steps – suddenly expand until the edges are a million miles away, then a trillion, and then ... cease to exist. My iPhone, which once appeared omniscient is exposed as merely a child's walkie-talkie. My high-definition camera turns out to capture reality about as well as a stick drawing. This is the realm beyond apps, for which Wikipedia has no answers, and where even the most high-brow of academic journals are just a fumble in the dark.

This is awe.

This is the inability to comprehend how a new life, with a heart and a mind and a soul could come from two cells haphazardly meeting. This is falling in love, feeling like the arms which hold you are the only home you'll ever need. This is sunsets that paint a whole sky with shades of pink and orange and red you never knew existed; mountain ranges whose soaring heights bring to mind how we are all tiny specks on a timeline which stretches beyond our ken; or just the quiet moment when spring air slips past you after a long, dark winter and reminds you that new life is just below the surface. And, with each of these encounters with transcendence, you know that none of this comes from our will and design. That all of it, every last inch and every single drop of it is grace.

We could rephrase God's response to Job this way then: 'The best, most glorious thing that has happened in your life – could you have created it, masterminded it, even expected it?

No? Then why are you interested in control? Has control ever expanded your heart, lifted your spirits or filled you with joy? Life and love cannot be programmed or pre-planned – they defy the laws of cause and effect. It is all gift, pure gift, from me to you. You don't need to try to squeeze into the driver's seat: trust me, I know what I'm doing. I've got this; I've got you.'

So, no, my attempt at twisting God's arm so that I could live a quiet and easy life did not go to plan. I would say since becoming a Christian, I've felt the floor fall out from beneath my feet a fair few times as I've lost jobs and relationships, been weighed down with depression and made breathless by anxiety. Illness, death and divorce have hurt the people I love most and left me scrambling for answers and glimmers of hope. And I have felt the quiet pain and dull grief of false starts, of frustrated hopes, of not quite living up to expectations – the ones I had for my own life and the ones that others had for me.

But I have come to trust that God has not been punishing me. It is not God withdrawing from me. It is not God forgetting me. I don't always know, at the time or afterwards, what He is doing or what part spiritual warfare has to play in each iceberg I hit. God is seemingly unselfconscious about leaving an excruciating amount as mystery. He will not necessarily tell us in advance how He will be at work in the maelstrom but unexpected, and even painful, twists and turns are never ones we make alone – they always fall in the footsteps of love and faithfulness incarnate.

For when Jesus called the disciples to 'follow' him, He meant it quite literally. The disciples were to fall in step with Jesus on a journey he was already on – a three-year-long journey which would end not in a victory lap or military procession, but trudging up to Golgotha, the place of the skull. They would learn from him, and what it meant to trust him, not through an in-depth induction or a strategy away day, along the way. And the same goes for us: we don't get all the answers we'll ever want before we set out, but as we go. And sometimes we get just enough to keep going.

What you see and live through and discover will not always point clearly to God's goodness. The Bible is a tear-stained book: virtually all the heroes of the faith, including Jesus himself, weep over the gulf between the world as it is and as it should be. But this is faith – going down into the depths, all the way down, sharing in Jesus' death, assured that you will re-surface, that he will pull you up into his resurrection life. Faith, regrettably is not synonymous with certainty for, unlike certitude, it always involves vulnerability – the giving of oneself to another and the surrender of all efforts at controlling what happens next. So even in my unknowing, I choose to hope and trust that God is love, that He is for us and not against us and that He will never abandon us.

2. There's no such thing as a free lunch

Have people always been this exhausted? On my way to work, the tube is crammed with people with their eyes closed, even if they're standing up. I only know this because occasionally I open mine. An addiction to caffeine is now the default, and the only other socially accepted response besides 'good, thanks!' when someone asks how you are is 'urgh, knackered'. The inquirer nods knowingly and there is a brief moment of bonding over your mutual fatigue.

We Brits are happy to make an exception to the usual rule of keeping public displays of emotion to a minimum when it comes to tiredness because it's become something of a status symbol. Whereas in centuries gone by, long hours were associated with farm hands and factory workers – the working classes – in our achievement society, they're the stuff of the business elite, bankers, consultants and lawyers who stay in the office long past midnight and can't remember the last time they had a weekend. And somehow, that's something to boast about: if you're tired, you must have to work hard because you're in demand, and so, the myth runs, you must be especially valuable. Dark circles around the eyes are a badge of honour.

But why is everyone striving to prove their industriousness, even at cost to their own wellbeing? Because British society, like much of the West, is ostensibly meritocratic: the most talented and the most diligent are supposed to be able to climb to the top of the ladder no matter which rung they started on. We applaud people who make their own way in the world, especially when all the odds are stacked against them, more than those who have everything handed to them on a plate. In practice, of course, things rarely work out that way and there are plenty of obstacles to social mobility. But we grew up with the message that we could do anything we wanted and accomplish whatever we set our minds to. The world, we were told, was our oyster. So it is easy to overlook any structural barriers to us fulfilling our potential, and assume the fault is entirely ours if we don't rise to the top.

If it's assumed that everyone's position in the hierarchy is decided purely by their capabilities and not their circumstances, then our jobs market is one big survival of the fittest in which the individual and their 'selfish genes' are pitched against all others. There is no room for altruism, helping others up, or cooperation; everyone else is your competition. You might use them to get to where you want but you shouldn't feel obliged for, or beholden to, them. And nor will they do the same for you. It's a Darwinian dog-eat-dog world. So, to avoid being gobbled up or left behind, we have to continually strive to be more productive, more efficient, with our measurable outputs increasing all the time – not least because the ageism in our society means that if we don't make it big in our twenties, we're sure we will have missed the boat. Wisdom gained over years of experience means far less than it should when there's a nationwide allergy to wrinkles.

Unfortunately, it's not even like we can confine our time on the treadmill to ten hours a day, five days a week. Because the digital revolution, at the same time as empowering us in all kinds of ways, has also handcuffed us to our devices – so tightly that the boundary between our minds and our machines has begun to blur. We've outsourced our memory to Google and our reminiscences to digital photo streams, our decision-making to algorithms and our inquisitiveness to virtual assistants. As if we were the electronic devices to which we are glued (notice how often people talk about the way they are 'wired'), we are expected to 'be on' from 6am until midnight and to regard our home lives and personal needs as something of an awkward superfluous addition. Everyone knows we all have our mobiles within arm's length at all times so we feel obliged to respond to the emails which continually ping through the second they land in our inbox. Otherwise our commitment to the cause or the company might be suspect and we feel we can't afford to give the impression that we are anything besides a perfectly streamlined worker, with no other obligations or identities besides 'employee'.

The need to take care of our own mental and physical health as well as our friends and family sits awkwardly in the backseat, getting the snippets of our attention which we can afford to give without provoking an eye roll from our boss. Because when the most important value – in fact, the lens through which everything else is viewed – in our society is economic, only the quantifiable counts. And with everything measurable – from steps to calories, likes to sales – there is the inescapable sense that the numbers could be always better. 'Optimised'. Being able to collect so much data gives us the sense of being in control and the reassuring (albeit misleading) feeling of objectivity. But it also prompts us to forget or 'devalue' the things we cannot quantify.

We are not purely victims in this pressure-cooker though; in a funny way, we are also complicit in turning up the heat. Because even as we crave silence and stillness, and long to stop, just for a minute, just for once, that prospect also terrifies us. I run on distraction, using constant activity as a way of escaping my feelings, my insecurities and anxieties. With my professional face on, I don't have to look into my deepest wounds or listen to ghosts from the past. I never know when they might pop their head around the door and demand to be reckoned with. So rather than give them an opportunity to pounce on a quiet moment, I pack my diary full. Tired? Sure. Stressed? Definitely. But at least the big what-ifs are held at bay; existential angst drowned out by a constant buzz of videos, tweets, articles, songs, podcasts, playlists and anything else I can stream.

We're also tied down to the treadmill by our attempts to quell the lurking fear that we don't really fit in. The unique interplay of guilt, fear and shame that is imposter syndrome is something I know all too well. From Cambridge to Parliament, I have found myself in environments I never thought I would be, and where I have never felt like I – with my comprehensive school education, my Midlands accent, my repeated habit of having my skirt tucked into my underwear, and my lack of training in all things etiquette and decorum – belonged.

It was by some miracle that I even got into university. I was at my thinnest and my most terrified of the outside world. The last thing I needed was the stress of an interview for one of the most competitive application processes in the world. The college was teeming with exuberant bright young things, but I didn't dare speak to anyone. I didn't even dare look them in the face. It was the middle of winter so I was perishingly cold, and my bones felt like ice, making every movement excruciating. I had to put on make-up to look reasonably close to my age but it hovered above my ghost-pale skin. It looked more like a death mask.

When my mum came to pick me up – because we knew I would be too weak to get the train back by myself – she saw a crowd of bouncing, energetic girls who looked right at home. As if they had strolled off the polo pitch, she said. And then there was me: sticking out like a sore thumb. My clothes hanging limply off my frame. Drained, dark-circled, shaking with a deathly combination of fear and cold. Her heart sank. Studying at Cambridge had been my dream ever since I was six. If I didn't get in, if I lost my one ambition besides weight loss, there was no telling what I would do.

A month later, a letter arrived through the post. I was accepted. But for the next three years I never felt it.

So, when I arrived, I worked constantly, trying frantically to avoid having to face a results sheet that proved my suspicions: option a) I got in on a fluke; option b) I was fulfilling some quota for comprehensive schooled kids from north of the M25; option c) they felt sorry for me. I counted minutes like I had counted calories – each and every one had to be devoted to my degree. Just like I had panicked if I ate one bite more than I thought I should, if I 'wasted' a single second I would hyperventilate and descend into a spiral of self-loathing. Why was the queue at Sainsburys so interminably long? Why were the traffic lights always red when I cycled back from the library? How stupid did I have to be to think I had time to have coffee with my sister?

I was still living on a tightrope, but the terror that lay on either side was now not only becoming overweight but also failing my degree. Even when I was back home for the holidays, I spent every day, morning until night, crouched over a desk, with the heating turned off so that the chill would force me to focus. Taking Christmas Day off felt like a reckless indulgence. And when my mum tried to take me for a day out, I accused her of jeopardising my chance at a first. Loudly. In public. Perfectionism again blinded me to love. And while most people meet their closest friends at university, I never let anyone in. I was too scared of being found out.

I could never let up because I was only ever as good as my next performance – and I never knew how high the bar might be set. I might have handed the last essay in on time but the next reading list might overwhelm me unless I tried to pre-empt what it would contain before it had even been released. I might have passed my last exam but what if the next one covered a topic I forgot to revise? It was not that I just had panic attacks: anxiety racked my every cell for three whole years.

Whenever you are trying to earn your place, the goalposts are always prone to shift. Because each time you level up, you find there are new hierarchies to climb and deeper inner circles to unlock. This stage might have once looked like 'the one', but nevertheless, you find yourself drawn to the next rung, and the one after that, and the one after that. The feeling of having arrived is always a contemptuous whisper out of reach. And once you assume that everything worth having requires hustling, that mind-set tends to spread beyond the 9-to-5 (or 8-to-8 as the case may be) to colonise other areas of your life.

I think that might be behind the tendency to put on a pedestal the people who least recognise our value and to focus on winning *them* over while pushing away those who already appreciate us. The warped reasoning runs that if we are as unlovable as we suspect, then anyone who wants to spend time with us as we are must be even more flawed. Or as Groucho Marx put it 'I wouldn't belong to any club which would have me as a member'.

The feeling that we have to bend over backwards for something which is already in our hands can certainly affect how we relate to God. I thought that I had to pay God back for my salvation and to give Him a good return on his investment, so to speak. And often I feared that God's love was gradated, and to climb up the ranks, or to avoid losing it altogether, I had to achieve something awe-inspiring which brought Him glory. Because although we might *say* that God loves everyone and that His love is unconditional, deep down there is the suspicion that God prefers those who fit a certain set of criteria – whether it relates to sexual orientation, political leaning, or how they spend their time and money. Or we might verbally profess that we are all equal because we are all saved solely by grace and not by works, but with our social cues we suggest that those who excel at evangelism, who work full-time for Christian charities and, most of all, celebrity preachers and pastors are, in fact, higher in the spiritual pecking order.

For a couple of years after leaving university, then, I was caught up in something between survivor's guilt and a second messiah complex. I had spent my early life as a Christian in circles where one of the battle-cries was 'take culture back for Christ': in addition to evangelising individual people, we were looking for ways to engineer society in such a way as to make Christianity more plausible and acceptable, and its ethics the default way of living for those of all beliefs and none. I felt a huge responsibility to do exactly this, single-handedly of course, to prove to God that I was worth having on board. But I couldn't figure out how to go about it or what strategy would have guaranteed results, and I was terrified of wasting the time God had given me. I felt like God was standing far in the distance, expecting me to somehow reverse secularisation but giving me no pointers on how to do so. And, surprisingly enough, those jobs with the greatest reach and impact weren't open to recent graduates with a history degree and a chip on their shoulder. Weird.

I felt one passage from the Bible in particular breathing down my neck: the Parable of the Talents. In that story, a master puts his servants in charge of his assets (talents being a measure of money) while he goes away for a trip. On his return, he assesses how well they have invested the amount they were given, and because of the faithfulness of the two servants who return with a profit, they are rewarded by being given stewardship over even more. The third servant, though, who plays it safe by burying his talent in the ground, is punished.

When I read this passage, I was sure this was the verdict I would receive: I could almost hear God listing all the privileges into which I had been born and those I had accrued on the way and, in another column, listing the number of people I had managed to convert or the policy changes I had achieved. The sum total? Nothing. Nada. Zilch. I would have nothing to show for having been born into the middle class in one of the richest countries in the world, and having been given a prestigious education to boot. I lived in terror of that reckoning.

But, looking back, I think I had got the wrong end of the stick when it came to this parable. When the third servant explains why he buried his talent in the ground, he says: 'I knew that you were a hard man, harvesting where you did not sow, and gathering where you did not scatter seed, so I was afraid' (Matthew 25:24). The master flips, angry at having been accused of profiting from others' labour, essentially being characterised as a mafia boss. At the core of this story, then, is one's perception of the master, because we have a way of imitating the image of God we have in our minds. If you believe that God is self-serving, you will likely look to your own interests too and treat God as someone with whom you do business deals, but not someone to whom you give your heart. And, if you believe that God is looking to trip you up, then you are bound to live cagily and cautiously – an outlook which fits poorly with the inherently risky journey which is following Jesus.

It is risky to turn the other cheek – what if your attacker slaps you on the other one too, and kicks you in the kneecaps for good measure? It is risky to choose peace – what if your enemy doesn't put down their weapon? It is risky to be radically hospitable – what if you're taken for a ride? It is risky to 'sell all your possessions and give to the poor' (Luke 12:13) and rely on God's provision – what if no one shows you the same generosity? We aren't ever guaranteed that imitating Jesus will go smoothly – as the martyrdom of the apostles, John the Baptist, and Jesus himself testifies. But it is by wandering into unknown territory that we most grow as people, and become the fullest version of ourselves. God is forever calling us out of our comfort zones.

My safety blanket is books. In books, even the weightiest of concepts and the unruliest of narratives get neatly distilled, packaged up and footnoted. So, for me, it's far easier to absorb the right answers from the right reading list than to live this bold, eyebrow-raising cross-shaped way of life. Far easier to concern myself with the state of the hearts of those people over there than my own. Far easier to point out the specks in their eyes (and even design a special awareness campaign around said specks) while leaving the giant sequoia in my own eye untouched.

I was using the mission of changing the world as a diversion from getting my own moral compass set straight. I wanted to be able to skip a level – to produce a piece of legislation, policy report or some such – that could make the world a better place without having to address how my self-centredness made me part of the very problems which plague our planet. Until our own internal cosmos is oriented rightly, every attempt at transforming the world beyond ourselves will be built on shaky ground and hot air.

Trying to ground my righteousness on having all my doctrinal ducks in a row and a proof-text for every theological conundrum was equally misplaced. Jesus said we needed to 'receive the kingdom of God like a little child' or we'd never be able to enter it (Luke 18:17). That doesn't mean we need to disengage our brains whenever we set foot in church, but I think it does speak to why we seek, and how we use, knowledge. Children love learning; they bubble over with questions about the world. But they don't see knowledge as power, in the sense of something which they can use against others, which can set them apart and aloof or earn them status and superiority. Whereas I was stocking up on books and memorising lectures so that God couldn't accuse me of heresy (and so I'd be able to sit in smug judgement on the orthodoxy or otherwise of other people's views), children learn from a place of fascination not fear.

So, if anything, my terror of the Parable of the Talents put me directly in the shoes of the character I was anxious I might end up playing, but not for the reasons I imagined. It wasn't because I failed to give God a good return on His investment, but because I had imagined Him as miserly and menacing. In my assumption that God would be most interested in the information which appears on my tax return and LinkedIn profile, I had forgotten that He knows the very fabric of our being, our every thought and heartbeat, and so isn't all that preoccupied with our ninety-word bios. I worried that God would direct me by barking steps one to three thousand, enough to last my entire lifetime, in one go and, if I missed the lecture or failed to memorise each instruction correctly, would tut 'sorry, I don't do repeats'. But, in reality, God guides as a shepherd: in the here and now, step by meandering step.

There isn't a divine flow-chart which we have to discern at the moment we graduate from university; we have to do something both more simple and more demanding: attend to God's presence moment by moment as we seek to love Him and love others in the humdrum as well as the milestones. The journey is, after all, not a way for us to reach a God standing off at an aloof distance, but something which He wants us to join Him on.

My reading of the Parable of the Talents also revealed my pride, concealed under a layer of low self-esteem. I had forgotten that the Kingdom of God (the areas of life, of our minds and actions, where God's will is enacted) is spread not by top-down imposed change devised by powerful humans, but from tiny mustard seed-sized beginnings quietly enlivened by the Spirit of God in ways beyond human understanding let alone control. So I was turning my nose up at anything that wouldn't obviously affect change on a national scale. But whereas our culture is preoccupied with productivity and maximising impact, the Parable of the Talents actually shows God to be far more concerned with faithfulness – and faithfulness, to be sincere, has to always include the small things.

I could, for example, establish a charity, and still look at the world with cynicism rather than hope. I could give away all my worldly wealth but withhold forgiveness from those who have wronged me. I could embark on a whole sweep of mission trips but pour scorn on those who think differently from me. And no matter how impressive it all looked, the Kingdom of God would not have grown one millimetre.

Far from standing to one side while we jump through a series of hoops to prove our worth, the initiative always comes from God. Because God created us out of, and for, love. That means whatever we do *for* Him we also do *with* Him. We were loved before we had done anything to earn it. Take Mary, for example.

What made her worthy of bearing the Son of God? What possibly *could* have made her worthy? Was she the most virtuous young girl that ever lived? Had she particularly excelled at minding her Ps and Qs? Not according to the song of praise she sings after hearing she will give birth to the Messiah:

My soul magnifies the Lord,
and my spirit rejoices in God my Saviour,
for he has looked with favour on the lowliness of his servant.
Surely, from now on all generations will call me blessed.
(Luke 1:46–48)

God had looked not on her self-discipline or her outstanding moral character, but her lowliness. 'Hail Mary, full of *grace'*, the prayer goes; not 'Hail Mary, full of merit' or 'Hail Mary, full of potential'. Our weaknesses, those things which exasperate us, the ones we try to expunge from our existence, are God's inroads.

If this is something you struggle to get your head around, you aren't alone: Paul had to wrestle with it too. When he confronted a 'thorn in the flesh', he begged God three times to take it away (2 Corinthians 12:7). We don't know what Paul was referring to – maybe an illness, memory of past guilt, or a repeated struggle against temptation – but we do know from another of his letters that he was frustrated with his own proclivity to fall into sinful patterns when he knew better (Romans 7:19). Rather than plucking out the metaphorical thorn, God responds 'My grace is sufficient for you, for my power is made perfect in weakness.' So, Paul resolves to 'boast all the more gladly about my weaknesses, so that Christ's power may rest on me' (2 Corinthians 12:9).

This can't have been easy given that Paul's religious heritage and spiritual CV were impeccable. But, as he followed Jesus, he had to embrace a different perspective on every achievement and credential which had formerly made him feel significant. Paul had to continually die to his old habit of thinking that he could earn God's blessing and, like Mary, magnify the Lord instead of zooming in on his own contribution. 'If someone else thinks they have reasons to put confidence in the flesh', by which he meant confidence in their own efforts – external and internal,

> I have more: circumcised on the eighth day, of the people of Israel, of the tribe of Benjamin, a Hebrew of Hebrews; in regard to the law, a Pharisee; as for zeal, persecuting the church; as for righteousness based on the law, faultless. But whatever were gains to me I now consider loss for the sake of Christ [...] I consider them garbage, that I may gain Christ and be found in him, not having a righteousness of my own that comes from the law, but that which is through faith in Christ—the righteousness that comes from God on the basis of faith. (Philippians 3:1–10)

If God was in the business of asking us to earn His blessing, then Paul had every reason to be confident. He was circumcised in accordance with Levitical law; an heir to God's covenants with Abraham, Isaac, and Jacob; from one of Israel's most distinguished tribes; and unashamed of his Hebrew heritage. As a Pharisee, Paul was one of the elite group known for their scrupulous devotion to God's law and for radically separating themselves from anything deemed unclean. Plus, he had not even just waged *intellectual* war against perceived heresies: he had actively persecuted the so-called Christians. If it was possible to attain righteousness by one's own hard work, Paul was in the clear. But, he had learned, it wasn't.

Even as he wrote this letter from prison, having lost all his possessions, his status, his liberty and probably his family because of his newfound faith, he still maintained that the very things that had once made him feel safe and superior had in fact come at a cost. Instead of having brought him closer to God, by stoking up his own sense of pride, they had prevented Paul from seeing God as the God of grace.

You might delay respecting yourself until you can Polyfilla in the cracks in your character, but they don't alter God's love for you one jot. You might resent, fear, and shame yourself for the ways in which you do not live up to your own expectations, let alone God's. But when God welcomed you into His family and set His own Spirit in you, He was under no false impressions about your strengths and weaknesses, your waywardness and your blunders. He knew this wasn't a deal that left Him with the upper hand.

You might have learned to expect quid pro quos or to come against hard boundaries to people's generosity, patience and mercy. But unlike us created beings, who inconsistently embody even our most defining traits and characteristics, God is not just loving and gracious but *is* love and grace. They are His essence – His very nature which He cannot act against. In a world which tells us everything has to be earned – self-esteem, love, as well as everything with a barcode – God's mercy, blessing, healing and restoration are all given freely and undeservedly.

As with Mary, it was those who, from an outside perspective, had very little to give who Jesus pronounced as blessed or whose faith he praised. The very first in the Beatitudes are the spiritually poor – those who totally lacked Paul's religious zeal and ancestry. And while Paul had not compromised with the surrounding Greek culture and removed himself from anything ceremonially unclean, Jesus once described as 'justified before God' a tax-collector, who, since he profited from collecting tax for the Romans, would have been seen as the archetypal turncoat, someone willing to put personal gain above loyalty to his people.

To some who were confident of their own righteousness

and looked down on everyone else, Jesus told this parable: Two men went up to the temple to pray, one a Pharisee and the other a tax collector. The Pharisee stood by himself and prayed: 'God, I thank you that I am not like other people — robbers, evildoers, adulterers — or even like this tax collector. I fast twice a week and give a tenth of all I get.' But the tax collector stood at a distance. He would not even look up to heaven, but beat his breast and said, 'God, have mercy on me, a sinner.' I tell you that this man, rather than the other, went home justified before God. For all those who exalt themselves will be humbled, and those who humble themselves will be exalted. (Luke 18:9–14)

Only when we can look honestly at ourselves, facing up to all our imperfections, can we really appreciate how much God loves us, and have a proper taste of His mercy and loving kindness. That's why confession precedes communion. Our weakness does not disqualify us from God drawing near – acknowledging our finitude and our failures is actually a precondition for it. Because how can we truly worship God when we are busy praising ourselves? How can we die to ourselves and entrust all that we have to God if we reckon we have a pretty decent track record, thank you very much? And how are we supposed to truly love others, and even consider them as more significant than ourselves, when we are meticulously marking out our achievements compared to theirs?

As soon as we think we have brought something to the table to present to God, we are bound to start comparing our pot-luck offering with those which other people have brought. And once we do so, bitterness, envy, and arrogance will begin to crowd our hearts. It doesn't matter if you're judging others for being left-wing or right-wing, for their sexual orientation or for not recycling, for skipping Sundays or for street-preaching, if you think your behaviour or beliefs mean you deserve something that others don't, then you risk letting grace slip through your fingers. Even if we start being glad of our own humility, while pitying those who remain blinded by their own arrogance, we've been caught out again. Ego is a devious little thing, sneaking up on us when we least want it to and leaving us always, always in need of mercy.

In Jesus' parables, the characters that try to get their just deserts by playing by the book end up resenting the figure symbolising God. In the Parable of the Prodigal Son, for instance, the elder brother is furious when his father welcomes back the profligate younger son with open arms. In a huff, the elder brother refuses to go to the celebratory party.

So his father went out and pleaded with him. But he answered his father, 'Look! All these years I've been slaving for you and never disobeyed your orders. Yet you never gave me even a young goat so I could celebrate with my friends. But when this son of yours who has squandered your property with prostitutes comes home, you kill the fattened calf for him!' 'My son,' the father said, 'you are always with me, and everything I have is yours.'

For the elder brother, closeness to his father was of little value: he had his eyes set on what he could earn for himself by playing the good guy. He was as self-interested as the prodigal son had been – he simply had a different game-plan for getting what he wanted. And while the younger brother had come to the end of himself and got a glimpse of the radical mercy and generosity of his father, the elder was disgusted by such kindness.

In God's economy, then, those who want to make a show of their piety and those who want to assert their superiority are the ones who risk losing everything. They're the ones who risk accidentally rejecting God not because they don't believe He exists, but because they want to insist on a division between deserving and undeserving – the very wall which God wants to break down. If God has said it all comes down to grace, then it is not for us to add caveats and clauses. That most famous verse, John 3:16, tells us that 'God so loved the world that he gave his one and only Son, that whoever believes in him shall not perish but have eternal life.' God did not lend, take or demand: He gave, He sacrificed, He shouldered all the cost.

God, you see, holds nothing back. Having given you His very self in the form of His Spirit, the most precious, the eternal, the divine has already been planted in you. It is already yours to breathe in and relish. What, in heaven or on earth, could there be left to work for? What could there possibly be to add? That Spirit, Paul says, is a seal, 'a deposit guaranteeing our inheritance until the redemption of those who are God's possession' (Ephesians 1:14). It's a done thing. You've nowhere else to get on that treadmill of yours: you've already arrived.

3. Keeping up appearances

We were told not to judge books by their covers when we were little, weren't we? We had school assemblies about how beauty was skin deep and how it was very naughty indeed to call kids names based on their appearance. But children have a good nose for hypocrisy. Even before you've begun to stretch your critical thinking muscles, you can tell when the adults in the room are setting rules for the little ones that they have no intention of heeding themselves. You watch grown-ups have their pudding without finishing all their vegetables, run down the stairs in socks, and use bad language when they think you can't hear. It's the same with the lesson about making judgements based on appearances: we figured out pretty quickly that that wasn't the way the world really worked.

We saw films where there were visual cues for good, bad and foolish characters. The goodies beamed their innocence, dressed as impeccably as their personal ethic; the baddies sneered and were (problematically, of course) associated with darker colours; and the village idiot characters had bug eyes and bad dress sense. We saw music videos where the women who posed, dressed and moved in a suggestive manner were the ones 'picked' by men who assumed the women were sexual objects existing solely for male gratification. We heard 'sexy' used as a synonym for good or exciting, and applied to everything from software to political slogans, as if sex appeal was the only draw something could ever have. And we saw make-over shows where a girl got her hair straightened, took off her glasses, had her braces removed and bam, she was all set to find true love.

We drank in the aspirations, the judgements and the fantasies which were not instinctively our own, but which cast a long shadow, shaping our thoughts, feelings and lives for decades to come. We learned to pinch our tummies and hold our breath. We learned phrases like 'cellulite', 'pear-shaped' and 'thigh gap', the different categories of noses – hawk, big, snub, button, ski-slope – and to mentally dissect our bodies into good bits and bad bits. We began to see our body not as a gift but as a project, with aspects to flaunt and 'problem areas' to improve. Bodies like businesses needed assessments, evaluations and strategies. Earlier, I described anorexia as centred on a need for control, and it is. But it cannot be separated from the pressure we all face to cultivate a certain image of ourselves, whether through changing our physical appearance or our online presence, to try to earn our place in the world. People make judgements about our character and our value based on first impressions and facades, and so, we learn to judge ourselves on our appearance too.

Better to get in there first, I have long presumed: better to pre-empt the criticisms other people might make so that if I ever do have to confront it head on, it won't come as a surprise. I'll have already heard those words, albeit in my own voice. This is, of course, nonsense: shaming is shaming, and turning yourself into your own worst enemy makes everything far more painful. But quite frankly, how else have women been taught to talk to themselves?

One of the only solutions to our self-esteem problems which we have been given is new products, different treatments, and improved techniques. Once you try these, it is suggested, you'll finally accept yourself and be universally adored to boot. But the reason the beauty industry in the US alone was valued in 2019 at $532 billion, and forecast to only increase, is simple: it is impossible to feel like you have ever done enough to meet its arbitrary standards. Likewise, the weight-loss and anti-ageing markets wouldn't both be worth hundreds of billions if their products actually worked in the long-term. Their profit margins rely on us having to keep coming back for more.

As much as certain companies now use the language of body

positivity to sell their products, they are ultimately dependent on your dissatisfaction with your current appearance – otherwise you would know that you don't need their powders and potions to be worthy of love. The truth is, someone is always profiting from your low self-esteem – which is why they surround you more than ever with highly edited pictures of unattainably beautiful women so that you start to see the borderline impossible as normal and yourself as far outside the bell curve.

I've spent over a decade feeling like a blight on the aesthetic landscape. When I first entered secondary school, I was the girl with all the 'boyfriends' (not that we ever spoke to each other, of course, but they would buy me a chocolate bar or a keyring and then we'd 'break up' the day after). I didn't have any qualms about my appearance then. But as we went into our second year, I slipped to the bottom of the pile. I didn't learn quickly enough how to do my hair or make-up. I was too interested in schoolwork. I still looked very much a girl and not like I was 12 going on 22. The boys I liked stopped liking me back. The Christmas country dancing lesson, the most awkward event of the school social calendar, came around and I was the only girl without a partner. I knew then that no matter what my mum said about me being beautiful, there must be something wrong with me after all.

And so, for the next couple of years I tried, and tried, and tried to get the attention of boys, thinking that if only I could be the one that they all wanted, I could accept myself again. But all I did was reduce myself to an object, and a disposable one at that. I saw myself as being on some sort of market and reasoned that if there were no bidders, I was clearly damaged goods. Instead of boosting my self-esteem, it was shredded to pieces.

This was a few years before the reign of smartphones and social networks began. So if it was possible, common even, to filter life and even one's own self-worth through a commercial lens then, it is infinitely easier to slip into such reductivism now.

The online world is an attention economy, where monetary value is attached to numbers of views, likes and follows. Content marketers verbally disassemble us, referring to us as 'eyeballs', which are then targeted and costed out. But although images in this media environment might be worth thousands of dollars as well as a thousand words, there's no guarantee that those words can actually be trusted.

Take Fyre Festival, billed as the ultimate in luxury experiences – a music festival in the Bahamas with tickets costing up to $25,000 – which turned into the wettest of damp squibs. Its promotional video featured supermodels lounging on tropical beaches and private yachts, interspersed with clips of musicians playing to enormous crowds and the promise of a location on an island once owned by Pablo Escobar, the kingpin of an infamous drugs cartel. The biggest social media influencers were all paid to tell their fans they would be attending, and their audiences were keen to follow suit – not least to have something extraordinary to share on their own feeds. But the build-up was established on something even less stable than Caribbean sand.

The island and the models in the promotional video were nowhere to be found at the actual festival. It was hosted in an abandoned development near a Sandals Resort instead of a secluded island. Guests had been promised accommodation in cutting edge geodesic domes but when they arrived, they were presented with the type of tents used in humanitarian crises – and there weren't even enough to go around. Of the advertised line-up of 33 artists, not a single one turned up. After a night of tropical rainfall, the event was cancelled leaving many guests stranded. No one would be cultivating their friends' envy with their social media posts after all.

When the documentaries about Fyre Festival came out in 2019, audiences were horrified and enraged at the organisers' hubris. But in the age of the online influencer, there's a little bit of Fyre in all of us. The pressure to be our own mini PR machines is overbearing: we aggressively promote ourselves and selectively broadcast particular aspects of our lives, forging a slick brand out of what is in reality a hodgepodge of ups and downs. It doesn't necessarily mean we are duplicitous, but no matter how 'authentic' a person appears to be, their social media feed is still a curated collection of moments they've chosen to publicise. Little of our contradictoriness, of our overthinking, of our regrets or the mundanity that is the much larger backdrop to our highlights reel makes it onto our front page to the world. We know how to use filters to heighten reality, how to photoshop ourselves into a smaller dress size and a whiter smile, and how to phrase a caption to present an interior in line with the polished exterior we have designed.

It's not that all of us are desperate to be famous. But with the constant encouragement to look like supermodels, eat like food critics, and holiday like wealthy socialites, taking your foot off the pedal and calling a time-out on competition is tantamount to disappearing off the map. You're either living your best life, or you are irrelevant. 'Pics or it didn't happen' essentially means that to demonstrate our existence has any kind of meaning and to prove that we are at all interesting, popular and dynamic, we have to obsessively record our experiences. So we orient our lives around what we can post on social media; we 'live for the gram'.

But it's not simply about trying to prove to *others* that we are significant. It wasn't until selfie mode that we could simultaneously see our reflection at the same time as record it – these devices and our social media profiles, which are essentially digital billboards of ourselves, encourage us to see ourselves in a whole new way. We try to represent the life we wish we had and propound self-propaganda in the images we post and the stories we tell about ourselves mostly in the hope, I think, that we will believe it ourselves, to win our own respect and admiration as much as anyone else's. Or maybe it's to convince ourselves that if we have their likes then we don't need their love.

But what really happens is we substitute other people's praise and plaudits for self-respect. So, the addiction deepens as we need new updates, reminders and notifications to tell us that we are still okay. And ironically, when we are fixating over what other people think of us, we are at our most *self*-centred, because we are only interested in other people insofar as they react to us in the way we have mapped out for them. We're objectifying them as much as we are objectifying ourselves.

That is the case even when the image of ourselves which we are trying to create isn't especially flattering. When I was recovering from anorexia, I wanted to stay thin so that I continued to look like a victim. If I looked weak and fragile, then people would have lower expectations of me, I could evade the responsibilities of adult life, and the failure I feared would follow if I tried to act my age. One time, I wanted to prove to someone who said my illness was all for attention that it wasn't all an act. So, I wore a low-cut shapeless dress which showed off my collar bones and the bones peeking through my chest. Because it was too thin to keep me warm, I paired it with winter boots and thick ski socks. I remember standing in front of a mirror, looking absurd, a cross between an ironing board and a snowman, hoping to myself that it would be inescapable for someone to notice that there was something drastically wrong with me; that it would inspire an apology, reams of sympathy and guilt. But it didn't. None of my painfully obvious signals were picked up. Again, an image might be worth a thousand words, but we cannot really determine which ones our 'audience' will actually hear.

My recovery also did not for a long time put an end to my feelings of shame and low self-worth, and this often meant a debilitating preoccupation with comparison. Wherever I went, my internal commentary was on full blast, assessing everyone I saw and how I ranked against them – were they prettier, did they look more confident, how well were they dressed? Everything was grist to the mill and absolutely everything was my business. I even tried to get inside their heads to work out what they were thinking about me. I bet he's wondering what someone so awkward is doing here; I bet she's asking herself what on earth I was thinking when I got dressed this morning; I bet they wish I'd disappear. In reality, of course, I wasn't occupying a single inch of their headspace. They had their own concerns, insecurities, and problems to wrangle with. They probably never even took a second look at me. It was the critical, degrading beliefs I had about myself which I was putting into their mouths.

Nevertheless, despite the fact that I was really waging battle with myself, I imagined these total strangers as my combatants in a war of words. In 'retaliation' I redirected my judgemental commentary at them instead – all in the interests of making myself feel safe. When establishing a proper foundation for a healthy level of self-esteem feels like such hard work, given the way the media continually highlights the ways in which you do not fit their conception of perfection, criticising others feels like a decent short-term solution. All it does, though, is keep the cycle of comparison in motion and fuel judgement at the expense of grace.

Which is why Jesus warned that 'in the same way you judge others, you will be judged, and with the measure you use, it will be measured to you' (Matthew 7:2). Since Jesus doesn't explicitly say *who* will judge us, it might not just be God who he is referring to but other people as well – as more people are drawn into playing tit for tat – and even ourselves, because the more we train our judgemental gaze, the more we subject ourselves to it. A common cultural motif paints God as a cantankerous old man, wagging His finger at us from a distant cloud, eager to mete out punishments for our disappointing track record. But an interesting implication of Jesus' teaching here is that it would be worse to be measured by our own standards.

Comparing ourselves to others only makes sense if we take

God and eternity out of the picture, thereby making other people the most important reference point and the current moment the only timescale of any significance. Imagine each individual plotted on a graph of success, as measured in human terms, and you'd be able to see differences between them with some plotted higher than others. But add God to the graph, and its scales would be blown apart. Compared to the source of all righteousness and goodness, the variation between us humans is utterly insignificant. None of us find ourselves somewhere on the chart where we do not need grace – the grace to empower us to do what we would otherwise not be capable of, and the grace of forgiveness when we inevitably fall short.

Lots of advice about comparison on the Internet will tell you to stay in your own lane because while someone you admire-slash-envy may be in a better place than you now, who knows what success lies around the corner for you, and (this part is whispered, implied, hidden between secret thoughts) who knows what roadblocks they might come across so that you can neatly overtake? While technically true, I don't think we should be secretly hoping for someone to fall at an upcoming hurdle so that we can pip them at the post. Since the very first rebellion, Satan has wanted to set us at odds with each other, to present success as a sum-zero game where one person's wins are another's losses, and so everyone is a competitor, a potential threat to our dreams coming true.

Gore Vidal once famously said 'whenever a friend succeeds, a little something in me dies'. But other people's happiness is not responsible for our pain. And whenever we think in terms of me versus you, or us versus them, the bitterness which rises in our throats whenever 'they' experience a win, starves our soul of what it most needs: love. As we shall see in the next chapter, blessings are not individual possessions to be hoarded, inventoried and contrasted with those of others; they are to be shared for the common good.

Finally, perhaps the most important reason we should avoiding judging others (and ourselves) is that, quite frankly, we suck at it. In *Thinking Fast and Slow*, behavioural psychologist Daniel Kahneman reveals how the 'law of least effort' applies to our attempts at making sense of the world and the terrifying extent of our fallibility – from believing something simply because we have heard it repeatedly to imagining causal connections without any evidence for them. One of the cognitive biases which Kahneman explains is the halo effect, whereby a person's positive impression of one aspect of something – bè it a situation, a person, brand or event – filters how they perceive another aspect of that object, or even the thing as a whole. So, for instance, for women especially, thinness is associated with self-discipline and being overweight is seen to signal a lack of willpower and laziness. This cognitive bias (and its flip-side, the horn effect) is how stereotypes and prejudice get played out in reality.

It is in a classic case of the halo versus horn effect that God famously utters, through his prophet Samuel, 'the Lord does not see as mortals see; they look on the outward appearance, but the Lord looks on the heart' (1 Samuel 16:7). In the ancient near east, kings had to be tall, attractive, strong, tried and tested on the battlefield, and, most importantly, the eldest son. Saul, Israel's first king, ticked all these boxes, but eventually it appeared that looks could be deceiving and God declared him unfit to be king. Nevertheless, even when choosing Saul's successor, Samuel was initially guided by the same superficial criteria. Old habits died hard.

To find Israel's next king, God sends Samuel to the house of a man called Jesse, and he organises a beauty pageant-cum-lineup of all of Jesse's sons. Samuel first sees the eldest, Eliab, and thinks, 'Surely the Lord's anointed is now before the Lord' (1 Samuel 16:6). But God tells Samuel not to trust his own judgement and instead to wait for a word from the Lord. Seven sons all pass by Samuel and it's one after another until he asks if Jesse has another son up his sleeve and the unlikeliest candidate, David, is brought to him. David is somewhat vertically challenged, with no military experience, and most shockingly for this culture, he's the youngest son. But, with no regard for those norms, God has him made king and the head of the line into which God's own Son will be born.

Choosing the overlooked and the unexpected is, after all, God's modus operandi. Throughout the Bible, he chooses the younger son over the elder. Slaves over Pharaohs. Outsiders over insiders. Wandering nomads, young unmarried peasant girls, and a ragtag bunch of fishermen over the religious and political elite. Unlike us, God does not depend on externalities. And while we rely on past experience to make evaluations about the present, God is able to see things afresh and solely for what they are. This is, after all, the essence of grace. When God tells us His mercies are new every morning, that He will forgive our sins and 'remember them no more' (Isaiah 43:25), He is reminding us that we too should be open to relinquishing old ideas, labels and associations – about other people and about ourselves.

And whereas, in this crowded attention economy, we feel like we have to fight to be noticed, God is not stingy with his attentiveness. Unlike humans, He does not bestow it only on the impressive and beautiful. In the Bible, the first name a human character gives to God is 'El Roi', which translates as 'the God who sees me'. And that name was given to him by Hagar, the slave woman owned by Abraham and Sarah. Having had her body used to bear a son for the couple, only to be further shamed and abused by Sarah, Hagar knew what it was like to be ignored, exploited and cast aside. But although she was made to feel worthless by those who considered themselves God's true followers, God found a way to show Hagar that she was not invisible.

When she was on the run from her master and mistress, an

angel met her in the desert to tell her that God had heard her misery and that she should call her son Ishmael, meaning 'God hears', so that she would never forget. She must have known then that God does not play favourites – His attention is not reserved only for those who could boast of wealth, power, status, or even an impressive religious vocation. He saw, and cared for, both sides of the feud. Neither side had to push the other down to win God's favour, for there is no sum-zero game with His love.

To feel truly seen though, you have to stand in your own skin – not one caked in cream or airbrushed free from blemishes. If you put on some sort of persona in order to be noticed and accepted, then it is a recipe for insecurity, resentment and sheer exhaustion later on. Questions like 'what would happen if I dropped the act?' and 'why does no one really love me for who I really am?' will reverberate until you curl up worn out, no longer sure of who you really are and burned out by playing the game.

When Jacob deceived his blind father, Isaac, to steal his brother Esau's blessing by dressing up in goats' skins to imitate Esau's hairy arms, I doubt that he actually *felt* blessed. I imagine he felt like a fraud, knowing deep down that this ruse would not end well. He was soon running for his life as Esau, unsurprisingly, was not too pleased that what should have been rightfully his had been stolen thanks to a bit of fancy dress. Jacob surely did not feel loved and chosen when his own twin wanted him dead.

Many years later, Jacob received another blessing – one which he could feel right in the core of his being. To get it, though, he had to wrestle with a mysterious angelic figure. He had to scramble about, in all his fleshy humanness, with someone far stronger than him. In that moment, there could be no hiding, no airs and graces, no pretence of being aloof and above it all. In short, there could be none of his usual pride. Jacob names the place of the contest Peniel, meaning 'face of God' 'because I saw God face to face, and yet my life was spared' (Genesis 32:30). To see God close up, Jacob's face had to be exposed; he had to take off his mask, his disguise, confronting and confessing who he truly was. Then, and only then, could he receive the blessing for which he had been hustling all his life.

Sometimes, we have to know we are viewed with unconditional love by someone else before we can dare look deeply at ourselves, warts and all. Otherwise, who knows if we will be able to live with what we find? That is, I think, why Peter had his most profound moment of conversion after he betrayed Jesus. Before that, Peter was pretty cocksure: he wasn't afraid to speak without thinking or to offer Jesus, his Lord and Saviour, instructions. He seems to have thought of himself as being fairly smart and deeply devoted. So, when Jesus told Peter that he would deny even knowing Jesus three times in one night, Peter couldn't get his head around it. The idea of being a traitor just didn't fit his self-image. But what Jesus saw more clearly was that Peter was torn between trusting Jesus and wanting to look like a success story. So, when it looked like he was going to be characterised as someone who'd wasted three years following a fraud, Peter tried to save his own skin.

As he lied about his connection to Jesus, Peter's fickleness and mixed motives must have been reverberating in his ears, and he surely realised that Jesus had known about them all along. The Peter who had struggled to accept that Jesus' victory would involve self-sacrifice had loved a version of the Messiah which was partly shaped by his own imagination and preconceptions. Jesus, however, had loved Peter exactly as he was.

So when the resurrected Christ appeared on the beach close to where Peter and his friends had spent a night trying to fish, Peter threw his concerns about appearances aside and jumped into the water to swim to shore. He was finally pursuing with unreserved passion the only thing that really matters: closeness to Jesus. And it is at this point, after Peter has given up on building *himself* up, that Jesus declared Peter would be the rock on which the Church will be established. It isn't any sign of success or trait about which Peter could boast that qualified him – he hadn't even been able to catch a single fish that night. Rather, it was his newfound humility, the recognition of his foolishness and his need for God's forgiveness.

It is because God sees truly and fully that Jesus warned us against cultivating a particular impression of ourselves, especially when it came to piety. Because to do so is to set the horizon of our gaze too low – on the eyes of others rather than of God – and prioritise their opinion of us over God's:

> Be careful not to practise your righteousness in front of others to be seen by them. If you do, you will have no reward from your Father in heaven. So when you give to the needy, do not announce it with trumpets, as the hypocrites do in the synagogues and on the streets, to be honoured by others. Truly I tell you, they have received their reward in full. But when you give to the needy, do not let your left hand know what your right hand is doing, so that your giving may be in secret. Then your Father, who sees what is done in secret, will reward you. (Matthew 6:1–4)

Likewise, Jesus urged his listeners not to pray in public 'to be seen by others' and when fasting, not to 'look sombre as the hypocrites do, for they disfigure their faces to show others they are fasting'. We should instead do these things for an audience of one as then 'your Father, who sees what is done in secret, will reward you' (Matthew 6:5, 16, 18). Wherever recognition and approval from those around us is our goal, that is, Jesus suggests, our sole reward.

When Jesus used the word 'hypocrite' here (Matthew 6:2), it did not mean someone saying one thing and doing another, as it does now: in the days of Ancient Greece and Rome, it referred to actors, who wore masks (you know the ones with the exaggerated grins or frowns from your primary school History lessons). It is likely, then, that when Jesus called the religious folk who make a big show and dance of their charity 'hypocrites', he was taking aim at the façade they were putting on, the stage-management they were conducting. And, quite frankly, how can you have an open and trusting relationship with God when you can't even be honest with yourself? Their very charade implies that they don't really believe in God, or at least in a God who knows them so deeply and intimately, since they think He can be fooled with a veneer.

It might be rarer nowadays to make a show of religious fasting, but I've never found an office kitchen or cafeteria where people aren't talking about the diets they're on, the ones they should be on, or the ones they're breaking. When I was trying to put on weight, and trying harder to *want to* put on weight, it was torturously tempting to be pulled back into my old ways by the common assumption that everyone *should* be trying to lose it. I think we talk so much about dieting because we want other people's reassurance that we are fine as we are, the encouragement which we no longer know how to give to ourselves. Maybe what we really want isn't to be thin per se: it's for other people's respect and admiration. So we contrive conversations in such a way as to provoke our friends and colleagues to tell us how good we look since we've started keto, or to reassure us that the world will probably not end because we ate that packet of crisps.

If they respond to our cues, then we might feel better – for a little while, at least – or we might not count it as valid given the pressure we effectively put on them. But either way, the unfortunate side-effect is that we feed into the very cultural norms which have inspired our unhappiness with our bodies in the first place. We have reinforced the normality of commenting on and policing each other's eating habits and appearance. So, it's only a matter of time before shame and judgement will again monopolise our inner monologue.

Jesus' teaching on charitable giving is also as relevant as ever. In fact, it's never been easier to virtue signal, to consciously demonstrate that we have the moral high ground. You don't have to set up a charitable foundation or establish a hospital wing in your name to have your philanthropy publicly recognised: online, you can share a petition you signed or avoid clicking 'anonymous' when you donate to your friend's fundraiser, and countless charitable campaigns play to our love of selfies by asking us to take one which promotes their message. But Jesus shines an uncomfortable light on our motives when we do so. Are we really looking to raise awareness of a cause or are we at least partly trying to raise awareness of our own righteousness?

Contrast our desire to always be seen in the best possible light ('would you mind deleting that picture of me? It makes me look like I have a double chin') with Jesus who, 'being in very nature God, did not consider equality with God something to be used to his own advantage; rather, he made himself nothing by taking the very nature of a servant [and] humbled himself by becoming obedient to death – even death on a cross!' (Philippians 2:6–8). Jesus could have, given the extent of his powers and his rightful claim to be worshipped, made sure everyone knew exactly who he was. Through his teaching and miracles, he could have made it so inescapably clear that he was God incarnate that no one had any choice but to worship him. But he didn't.

Jesus didn't fit anyone's expectations of how the Messiah would look and behave. He wasn't born in a palace, to a priestly line, and nor was he a warrior set about overthrowing the Romans by military force. Instead, he was born to a couple of nobodies, in scandalous circumstances, and, having spent his first years as a refugee, was brought up in a provincial backwater ('can anything good come from Nazareth!' was one of his disciples' initial objections to the idea that Jesus was someone special). He then lived in obscurity as a labourer for three decades, and after three years or so of ministry, was executed in the most shameful means imaginable as a common criminal. Nothing about his appearance or his background indicated that he was God's chosen one.

Even his own family were not fully sold on the idea that He was the Son of God. At one point, a crowd is gathered with him and 'when his family heard about this, they went to take charge of him, for they said, "He is out of his mind"' (Mark 3:21). Straight after, the teachers of the law – the very people who should have been the first to recognise God move – accused Jesus of being possessed by the devil and of performing miracles by demonic powers. The risk, then, of thinking we know what it would look like when God shows up, the risk of judging things to be holy or not based on our anticipations and preconceptions is that we might miss Him altogether.

The reason Jesus was willing to be misunderstood was because *he* knew exactly who he was and what God the Father thought and felt about him. At the beginning of his ministry, at his baptism, he heard the Father's voice declare 'this is my beloved Son with whom I am well pleased' (Matthew 3:17). That was enough to keep him from being shaken when Satan tried to sow seeds of doubt about his calling. And if Jesus could withstand those firing shots, then he certainly had nothing to fear from the lies and accusations of mere mortals.

Once you know that God sees it all and loves you anyway, then it doesn't quite matter what everyone else thinks. Which is why I love Paul's sass when he writes to the Corinthian church 'I care very little [...] if I am judged by you or by any human court. In fact, I do not even judge myself [...] It is the Lord who judges me' (1 Corinthians 4:3). Like Jesus, Paul came to trust that God's perspective on him – that he was blameless and beloved – was final, drowning out the chorus of criticism he faced from others and even himself.

That is what we have to hold fast onto, because while people around us are judging books by their covers (and reshaping those covers to conform to arbitrary beauty standards), God has a habit of defying appearances. In the Kingdom of Heaven, something as small and unremarkable as a mustard seed will grow until it stretches across the whole cosmos. In that Kingdom, we find our life by dying to ourselves. There, the first are last and the last are first. There, the outsiders who feel far from God are often closer to Him than are the religious types. There, pursuing the one is worth leaving behind the ninety-nine. There, the persecuted, spiritually worn out, and the grief-stricken are the blessed ones. And this Kingdom is built on a victory that looked like a failure, as Jesus overcame sin, death and the devil for the whole world by being bloodied, beaten, hung on a cross, just another plaything of the Roman imperial state. This is the topsy-turvy Kingdom, where you are continually caught off-guard by the God who loves to surprise and subvert expectations. Because what else could love do?

4. It's just me, myself and I

'No man is an island', John Donne wrote in a poetic meditation against isolationism in 1624. Three centuries later and I don't think we're any closer to coming to terms with the fact that we are all interdependent – 'a piece of the continent, / a part of the main', as Donne put it. Well, I certainly am reluctant to embrace that reality. Can't I at least be a peninsula, I wonder – connected to, and reliant on, as few people as possible?

With this musing I show myself to definitely be a product of Anglo-American culture which, since the 1970s especially, has been hyper-individualistic. Prime Minister Margaret Thatcher set the tone when she declared that 'there is no such thing as society'. If we do join groups or enter relationships, it is purely down to choice: we pick and choose friends, partners, clubs and churches like we do with any other consumer item. And if we feel we made the wrong choice, or they no longer meet our tastes and preferences, we detach ourselves and look for a substitution. Especially in a big city, with hundreds of fresh faces only an app away, it's easy to think anyone could be replaced with not too much bother. Single-use relationships to go alongside our single-use plastics and disposable coffee cups.

What is most important about us, according to this narrative, is not what binds us together or what we have in common, but what makes us stand out. Conformity is no longer a virtue: it's a death sentence. There's a reason why parents are desperate for their child to not share a name with anyone else in their class. There's a reason why everyone wants their wedding – that most age-old of ceremonies – to be different from anything their guests have ever seen, and their holidays to be light-years off the beaten track. And there's a reason why almost every product you can think of can be personalised. We want to feel special, like things were designed just for us.

In novels, movies and songs, history lessons and TV talent contests, we tend to tell the stories of individuals rather than collectives. It's all about their inner workings, their weak spots and their talents. We hear of great heroes who conquered whole countries; artistic geniuses whose oeuvres define an epoch; and celebrities who went from rags to riches as a result of their extraordinary gifts and hard work. Rather than seeing ourselves as swept up into some bigger story, one which long predates us and will far outlast us, we tend to think of ourselves as the stars of our own shows. As far as we are concerned, the clock started with the year of our birth.

This is admittedly the age of *social* networks and *social* media so we are supposedly more connected than ever. 'Bring the world closer together' became Facebook's mission statement in 2018. But the ironic thing about having the world, and the opportunity to connect with anyone in it, at your fingertips, is that it also makes it easier to keep them at arm's length. We can mute, unfollow, and undo just as easily as we can click like, follow and friend. And the more we have to up sticks and move, following the call of particular career ambitions or because the astronomical price of property prevents us from putting down roots, the more we have to stay in touch with our friends and family through a screen. Which means it is all the more easy to keep them on a need-to-know basis.

Deep bonds come from sharing experiences in the unfiltered flesh. They come from being open about what we are feeling in the moment, and letting someone see us unravel in real time (as opposed to telling them the story of our struggles after we've reached the light at the end of the tunnel). They come from being seen in the chaos, long before we've started to piece together how it all makes sense. These people can poke behind the image we project of ourselves. They aren't duped by our efforts at impression-management: they see too much to buy the two-dimensional version.

Having this kind of community, rather than just connections, is something that, as good as it sounds on paper, does not come naturally to me. The reality of not being able to determine how people see me and whether they like me feels like a thousand elastic bands being wrapped around my chest. I learned to keep my sadness to myself early on. Our family grew into a silently unhappy one with so much brushed under our communal carpet that it could be mistaken for the Himalayas. The sharp edges from the eggshells I was dared to stand on could have formed a similar silhouette. So, afraid of starting an avalanche, I found security in solitude.

I vividly remember a daydream of the perfect life I had when I was seven. Sat in class, I fantasised about living in a tiny tower, in which only I would fit, with a hatch through which I could receive schoolwork and hand it back once completed, meaning that my sole human contact would be the praise of my teacher. That was my idea of bliss. Oddly enough, I came very close to living it out at university, where I shut myself in my room for hours on end and worked obsessively in the hope that someone, anyone, would tell me I was good enough to be there. The reality felt more infernal than paradisiacal.

From a young age, I also self-soothed by building myself little dens that I could pretend were my real home. In winter, I would take a child-sized armchair, position it directly in front of my tiny artificial Christmas tree wrapped in fairy lights, and surround myself with the teddy bears I had commissioned myself to protect and the china dolls I had pronounced as friends – silently, stubbornly loyal. I would tell myself I was happy; I would tell myself I was safe. The spaces downstairs felt cavernous. The creak of the floorboards and all those myriad 'old house noises' betrayed an eerie silence. Here, with my red carpet underfoot, my room within a room felt knowable. What made it safe, I thought, was that it was just mine. It was reassuring to know that the grown-ups with all their secrets and surprises could not fit inside and upset its solitary order.

But those twelve steps to my bedroom were not enough to elevate me out of the minefield. When I was thirteen, my parents separated. My mum and I, who were left to rattle around the former family home after my sisters left for university, did not know how to talk about what had happened. We sat in our sadness in different rooms of the house, hoping that time would do the hard work for us. The room in which I holed myself up contained bookshelves full of self-help books. With their gaudy covers and bolshy titles, they promised that you could, with the right mantras, the right techniques, or the right gurus, have the career, love life, mind and body of your dreams. They all carried the same message: you don't need anyone else. All that was needed lay in those pages. But, as the growing library implicitly testified, finding the right book was a lifetime's work in and of itself.

Since then, the self-help and self-improvement industry has ballooned, and not only is it worth billions by itself, but it has also influenced the sales techniques for every other product under the sun. And of course, the blog posts and email newsletters have proliferated ad infinitum because the human need for answers, solutions and quick-fixes massively outweighs our aptitude for originality. The siren song is deafening whenever you go on Facebook or LinkedIn: 5 Ways to Be Your Own Hero; 3 Tips for Turning Failure Into Great Success; Why You Need to Be More and Do Less; and even, How to End Your Dependence On Other People (surprisingly, this last post didn't tell me how to cope without the people who make, transport and sell all the items I use each day, or those who manage and operate the public services on which I rely).

Especially around New Year, these '5 minute reads' promise a New You who is able to find time for multiple gym trips a week, twice-daily meditation and journaling sessions, and can balance setting up a start-up business with a full-time job and a happy relationship. All without breaking a sweat, thanks to the latest 'findings' from behavioural psychology and neuroscience which will maximise your productivity and willpower.

But the New You never shows her flaw-free face, partly because we don't run on software that can be so easily rewritten and upgraded. Quite frankly, if it took the death of God incarnate in order to save me from myself, a 600-word listicle is never going to cut the mustard. So, of course, we are left consuming more of this content as we keep slipping back into our old ways. And the sheer volume of videos, online coaches and e-books itself inspires anxiety of its own – namely, which New You should I become? There are too many sources of self-proclaimed wisdom to choose from: how do I know I've found the most nutritious diet or the workout routine with the quickest results? Should I read the guides that will show me how to get my ex back or should I watch the videos showing me how to get over him? And am I making my productivity system null and void by listening to too many podcasts about how to be productive?

It's peculiar that all this goes under the banner of *self-help* since it creates a dependence on these self-proclaimed authorities on the good life, even if the closest we ever come to them is a livestreamed seminar for the bargain price of $500. I understand the appeal of the term though. Watch the news and you can easily feel swept along by faceless, unfathomable forces – economic cycles, demographic shifts, climate change, global pandemics, geopolitical power plays. No wonder the promise of the self-help industry, that your personal choices decide the quality of your life, is so warmly welcomed. According to these secular priests, your salary isn't decided by a hypercompetitive globalised economy: it's determined by your attitude and your ability to sell your greatest 'asset' – yourself. The shape of your body has nothing to do with genetics, they counsel: it's all down to the perfect personal trainer, calorie counter and prepping your meals well. Find the right 'life hack' and all of life's mysteries can be decoded.

The idea that an individual's problems, and therefore the solutions, lie solely within themselves sounds delightfully straightforward, but it is sorely misguided. Our physical and mental well-being is largely influenced by factors outside ourselves, meaning we cannot simply flip a switch and suddenly find ourselves with a peppy, sunny-side-up, carpe diem attitude. The family you are born into – in terms of your genetic make-up, how well you were looked after, where you lived, your parents' relationship and income levels – can all impact your psychological well-being. As can, at a more macro-level, the amount of inequality in a society; the structure of the economy; the strength of the community and the quality of the physical environment around you. But all this complexity is pushed aside in order to present digestible proposals in a bullet-pointable format.

For instance, a go-to in the self-help world for anyone struggling with low self-esteem is positive self-affirmations. 'I have been given endless talents which I begin to utilise today'; 'I am the architect of my life and my potential to succeed is infinite'; 'I am loved and admired, and my value is recognised'; 'I am conquering my illness – I am defeating it every day'; 'I am indestructible – I can overcome any challenge'. Write them on a mirror, say them under your breath, play them to yourself while you drive or sleep and they will supposedly unlock the law of attraction, as made famous by Rhonda Byrne's *The Secret*. According to this law, the universe will give you whatever you focus your energy and attention on – send out negative energy into the universe with your anxieties, anger, or self-doubt, and you will attract more of the same. Alternatively, radiate confidence and visualise the success you wish to achieve, and like a magic genie, the universe will grant you your wishes.

Your thoughts, then, create reality: 'food cannot cause you to put on weight, unless you *think* it can', Byrne wrote. So, say you wanted to attract a husband, all you would need to do is visualise yourself coupled-up, experiencing romantic bliss, and act in such a way as to show the universe that you are ready to receive the gift it had in store for you: clear a space for Mr Right's clothes in your wardrobe, create a Pinterest board for your wedding and start saving for your first home together. Even people, then, can be controlled using just your imagination so that, like the china dolls and teddy bears I surrounded myself with as a child, they no longer carry the risk of free agents with their own unpredictable whims and wills.

But we can only fly so long in the face of reality before we crash back to earth with a bump. Since the universe does not exist at our beck and call, I can guarantee that the nutritional content of food, for example, will not change thanks to the powers of your imagination. And, more seriously, since love 'does not insist on its own way' (1 Corinthians 13:5) as Paul wrote, nor can a truly loving relationship come from coercion or manipulation: willing someone (even if just with your mind) to fulfil your desires is to treat them more as a possession than a partner.

Positive affirmations have also been found to be effective only for those who already have high self-esteem. For those of us with low self-confidence, they can actually make us feel worse because our mind intuitively grasps at all the reasons we disagree with the words that have been put in our mouths. If we were digital devices, we might be easily able to 'rewire' or 'reprogramme' our thoughts, like popular psychologists suggest. But as St Augustine wrote in his *Confessions*: 'The mind commands the body and is instantly obeyed. The mind commands itself and meets resistance.' That's something of an understatement in my experience: when I try to change how I think, I face the intransigence of an army of toddlers, the friction of rubber on rubber. The prescribed statements, telling myself how fantastic I am echo hollow in my ears. I don't believe them for one second.

Which is why one of my favourite days in the church calendar is Ash Wednesday: I kneel before a priest who makes the sign of a cross on my forehead with dirt and reminds me that I have come from dust and will return to dust, thoroughly dowsing the 'you got this!' vibe that the rest of the world tells me to exude. And yet I savour the moment. Because I don't have this. Not by a long shot.

One infamous feel-good mantra tells me that I am stronger than I seem, braver than I believe and smarter than I think. But (apologies to A.A. Milne who penned it) I'm not, and I have spent years keeping people at a distance so that they keep believing the hype I've constructed for myself as someone who has an answer for everything. Quite frankly, it is exhausting. So, hearing that God doesn't buy any of my self-propaganda, that I really am just human, and that He doesn't expect anything different, feels like being able to breathe in deeply after years of sucking in my stomach. Because what I really need to hear isn't that I am secretly awesome, but that in all my weakness, in my trepidation, and in my folly, I am loved.

In this individualistic setting, it is easy to feel bad about wanting, even needing, to be loved. With so much emphasis on self-care and self-love, and labels like 'high maintenance', 'needy' or 'thirsty' often used as gags, we can end up feeling like we should be able to meet all our own esteem needs, be our own biggest fan, have our own backs. Nothing epitomises this more than the rise of sologamy or self-marriage ceremonies, in which individuals marry themselves as a sign of their journey towards self-acceptance and apparent self-sufficiency. Maybe sick of broken promises, some people are choosing shelter in the only vow they think cannot be broken – one to themselves.

Autonomy doesn't just seem to be safer; it is also presented as what it means to be free – to be disconnected is to not be 'tied down'. 'You do you', right? This catchphrase of cultural and moral relativism implies that there's no need for rules or authority. But it can also be an excuse for apathy. If you're doing you and I'm doing me, then the sole thing that binds us is an agreement to not interfere in each other's lives.

When I was suffering with anorexia, I very badly wanted people to let me be and to stop interfering with 'the routine', to the extent that I barely left the house. Feeling like I could not cope with any more rejection, I pushed everyone else away. Love is unpredictable. Loving leaves you vulnerable: who knew if or when the other person would betray you, discard you, abandon you? Better, I thought, to shut people out. They're bound to leave eventually, I reasoned; this way at least I wouldn't be taken by surprise. Nothing hurts like getting your hopes up only to have them crash back down.

If anyone expressed concern about the weight I was losing, a voice in my head told me they were a filthy liar. 'They just want you to be fat,' it warned, 'they just want to feel better about themselves.' So, I learned to look upon them with suspicion. I became a stranger to everyone – not least myself. I remember standing in the corner of our kitchen, my mum gripping my shoulders, with horror in her eyes. 'Can't you see what you're doing to yourself!' she cried. In an almost out-of-body experience, I saw my face staring back at her: cold, possessed, as if a stranger to her. 'Everyone else thinks I look great,' I replied, perfectly numb to the pain I was causing her.

The voice of anorexia wanted full rein over my mind: it didn't want other people to sow seeds of doubt about whether my single-minded pursuit of thinness was really all that healthy, to show how much I had lost perspective, or to prove that I was loveable whatever my weight. It wanted, in other words, to surround me with falsehoods and distortion until I couldn't tell what was real. Slogans like 'live your truth' or 'what's true for you is true for you and what's true for me is true for me' suggest we can either reason our own way towards truth or, even better, create it for ourselves. But given my bent towards self-sabotage,

I know that I don't always have the clearest vision or the wisest strategies. My glasses are smudged with short-sightedness, biases, low self-esteem, and the belief that if I expect the worst, it won't hurt as much if my nightmare plays itself out in real time.

I thought the world would be a safer place if it was just me, myself and I, but actually the reverse is true. Not only can we combine our strengths and fill in each other's blind spots, but we also feel more confident when we look out onto the challenges which the world poses with someone else by our side. One study showed that individuals perceived a hill to be steeper if they were at the bottom alone, compared with if they were stood with, or even thinking about, a friend. Although we are used to hearing of heroes and heroines, individuals who made it against all odds, there is, in fact, strength in numbers. Research from psychology, biology and neuroscience all shows that we can't shake our need for community. Solitary confinement is one of the worst forms of punishment humans inflict on each other for a reason. We need to feel like we belong.

This need is not a weakness or an effect of the Fall; it is how we were made. When God first made Adam, He declared it 'not good for man to be alone' (Genesis 2:18) – not because it was a shame that Adam hadn't found the right girl yet, but because we are made in the image of God who is Himself community: God the Father, God the Son and God the Holy Spirit. Without people to give to and receive from, to love and be loved by, then, we would be something less than our true selves.

God makes the line between our reliance on Him and our reliance on each other nearly impossible to discern by often answering our prayers through the words and actions of other people. Rather than parachute supplies in from the heavenly realms to feed, shelter and protect those in need, He has always called his people to take care of the vulnerable and the outcast. Our interdependence, then, isn't something we are supposed to overcome or deny, contrary to what many self-help gurus would recommend, but something God calls us to lean into, accepting that we will sometimes be the ones in a position to help and, at others, the ones in need of support.

This contrasts starkly with the brutal underbelly to the law of attraction and much of the material produced under the banner of self-help: if everyone has the ability to change their world, then no one is responsible for anyone else. If superhero powers are inside all of us, we have no need to lean on, or support, anyone else. As Rhonda Byrne writes 'The only reason any person does not have enough money is because they are blocking money from coming to them with their thoughts.' Presumably this removes any obligation to give any money to charity and the most generous thing we could do for our friends is to buy them a copy of Byrne's book so they can unlock the powers within themselves. It might even take away our empathy for those who are suffering: humanitarian crises aren't, in this telling, so much caused by human pride, greed, or propensity to violence, or environmental disasters: they are apparently down to people sending out 'bad vibes' into the universe. Pushed to its logical conclusion, the law of attraction echoes Job's friends' response to suffering: it says they brought it on themselves.

Helping others isn't even considered a nice added extra to worshipping God: James made no bones about how faith could not just be about 'me and Jesus' when he wrote: 'Religion that God our Father accepts as pure and faultless is this: to look after orphans and widows in their distress and to keep oneself from being polluted by the world' (James 1:27). When asked which was *the* greatest commandment, Jesus sneakily responded with two: 'Love the Lord your God with all your heart and with all your soul and with all your mind. This is the first and greatest commandment. And the second is *just like* it: love your neighbour as yourself. All the law and the prophets hang on these two commandments' (Matthew 22:36 – 40). One isn't primary and the other secondary: in Jesus' mind, these commandments are unified; the call to social action, to seek justice and to be willing to make sacrifices is 'just like' the call to worship.

Loving others as God loves us means serving even those who cannot pay back the favour and those who are hard to love. We give because we have already received, not because we hope for further return. In a culture which idolises the streamlined, the most efficient, the 'lean and mean', this love which does not make a note of another person's slip-ups to use as leverage against them, this love which 'always protects, always trusts, always hopes, always perseveres' is truly a scandal (1 Corinthians 13:7). For there is something so wasteful about it – nothing flies in the face of economic rationality like 'I would do anything for you'. Yet it draws out the image of God in us – for God always honours the covenants He makes with humanity, no matter what it costs.

We see how this kind of commitment through thick and thin, better and worse, sickness and health, though 'wasteful' to an outside perspective, is used by God in the story of Ruth and Naomi. Naomi, her husband and her two sons had moved away to Moab, a foreign land whose people were much despised by the Israelites (according to Deuteronomy, no Moabite could enter the assembly of the Lord, even to the tenth generation, and the Israelites were commanded not to 'promote their welfare or prosperity'), to escape a famine in Israel. While there, the two sons married Moabite women, Orpah and Ruth. But then Naomi's own husband and both her sons pass away, leaving just the three women.

When Naomi gets word that the famine has ended, she plans to return to her home-town of Bethlehem and, aware that this would mean moving her daughters-in-law to another country where they would be reviled, she sets them free of their obligations to her. After all, widows were already at the bottom of the social pile – add the fact that they were from an enemy country to the mix, and it seemed they would be destined to be outcasts. So, she tells them to return to their families and prays that they will find new husbands.

Orpah accepts the considerate get-out but Ruth is having none of it:

> Do not urge me to leave you or to return from following you. For where you go I will go, and where you lodge I will lodge. Your people shall be my people, and your God my God. Where you die I will die, and there will I be buried. May the Lord do so to me and more also if anything but death parts me from you. (Ruth 1:16–17)

At first, Naomi resists, but eventually the two leave together for Israel.

I get why Naomi struggles to accept Ruth's loyalty – when I feel like I'm holding someone back or getting in the way, it is my pride as much as my compassion which means I want them to move on. In the stiff-upper-lip British culture where certain feelings are branded 'negative' or 'problem' emotions, I feel under great pressure to bring 'good vibes only' and, if I know that that's beyond me, I have a tendency to shut myself off for fear of 'infecting' anyone else. It feels safer to withdraw than to find our friendship was like a game Buckaroo, and my emotional baggage proved just too much.

But since God often works through other people in our lives, it is no surprise that Naomi's and Ruth's suffering is redeemed through their relationship. While gleaning to find food for herself and her mother-in-law, Ruth meets Boaz, a wealthy landowner and Naomi's distant relative, who is drawn to her kindness. The two marry and Boaz buys Naomi's land so that she too is provided for. Ruth, a Moabitess who could not enter the assembly of God, ends up as one of the five women in Jesus' genealogy. Through Naomi, she is well and truly brought into the family of God.

Like Ruth, we are called to incarnate the tenacity of God's

love and His steadfast loyalty. With our digital connections, it is easy to feel we can link up with people all over the world, but it is less common to feel responsible for, and dependent on, each other given that they effectively 'disappear' when we close our laptops. But the covenantal community into which we are baptised is not just a club: it is described as 'the body of Christ'. That means we can't just be acquaintances or Facebook friends: we are somehow, mysteriously and eternally bound to each other, joined together by divine tendons and ligaments. When you are part of a body, a living organism, there can be no going it alone. As Paul said, 'the eye cannot say to the hand, "I don't need you!" And the head cannot say to the feet, "I don't need you!"' (1 Corinthians 12:21). We are to 'carry each other's burdens' (Galatians 6:2) and 'mourn with those who mourn' (Romans 12:15). The boundaries between our lives are supposed to become blurred, as we become more sensitive to the needs and feelings of others, seeing them even as our own.

While I have been unable to scratch the surface of my own self-confidence, it has been other Christians who have incarnated God's love for me. My aversion to self-affirmations means I struggle to accept verses in the Bible which say I am beloved, a child of God, a co-heir with Christ. I can almost hear Satan's familiar phrase, the one which has succeeded at distancing us from God ever since the Garden of Eden: 'Did God really say...?' Did God really mean that to apply to you, Florence? Don't you think you're just reading other people's mail? I wish I could have the attitude of 'the Bible says it so I believe it', but when it comes to statements about my value in God's eyes – statements which go against the grain of everything I have told myself day in, day out for over two decades – I need a show as well as tell.

I think God knew we would all need each other to make tangible the verbal declarations of love He inspired. In his final words to his disciples, Jesus implores them to 'love one another' twice (John 13:34–35 and John 15:12). The first comes straight after telling them he will soon be leaving them: 'My children, I will be with you only a little longer. You will look for me, and just as I told the Jews, so I tell you now: Where I am going, you cannot come' (John 13:33). In other words, their love for each other is supposed to keep them strong and filled with hope even after Jesus is no longer physically with them. When God feels distant, when His love seems impossible, our love for each other is meant to fill the apparent gap.

When Jesus repeats this commandment, it is followed by a warning that the disciples will be hated and persecuted by the world because of their association with him (John 15:18–21). In this way, our love for each other is meant to make up for the sense of alienation we will feel when we choose to orient our lives around someone who many people think is a fictional character. Jesus also specifically told the disciples to love each other 'as I have loved you', perhaps referring to how he had just got on his knees and washed their feet. Jesus demonstrated to the disciples that the dirt and grime which they hid from the world did not deter him from drawing close, so neither should we be perturbed by the skeletons which lurk in each other's closets.

The reality that we are all part of a body also helps lift some of the burden put on our shoulders by our achievement society (and any messiah complex we might have picked up from church). Not only can none of us save the world single-handedly, but if we even try to, we will be avoiding the vulnerability, the ability to both give and receive love, that shaped even Jesus' own life.

God, the One who drew the whirl of the Milky Way did not need to whorl himself inside the womb of a young girl, dependent on her body for his growth and birthed in the same sweaty, bloody, undignified and yet somehow divine way that we all are. He didn't need to have been reliant on Mary and Joseph to feed, hold and bathe him, to teach him to talk, walk and read. Later, in his ministry, Jesus didn't need to work through people: he didn't need to send out the twelve and then the seventy-two, he didn't need to make Peter the rock on which he would build his church, he didn't need to ascend to heaven and leave us, with the help of the Spirit, to make disciples across the earth. He could have done it all himself, but he didn't. And if this was what the Almighty, the Alpha and Omega, chose, then real strength cannot mean self-sufficiency; it must mean trust, hope, and above all, love.

5. And they all lived happily ever after...

As odd as it might sound for someone in their twenties, I thought I'd have my happily ever after by now. I thought I'd be steadily climbing a career ladder, have my own place complete with Mr and Mrs towels to match a new moniker, and be free from all neuroses. I thought life followed the tripartite structure of Hollywood's films: set-up, development, resolution. In the first act, we'd meet the characters (with me, of course, in the starring role) and get a sense of the main conflict (my parents' divorce plus my teenage angst and insecurities). It would look like things were getting worse before they got better in the second act as an eating disorder entered stage left. But, in the third, all of those issues would be solved once and for all as the man of my dreams, who would help me accept myself, entered stage right and carried me off into the sunset.

Concerned that I might end up unexceptional and far out of the limelight, I even used to imagine my daily bus journey to school as the credits scene to my very own movie. I would imagine the camera starting at the front of the bus with all the children in view and then zooming in on me before cutting to a scene where something would trigger the dramatic narrative which would define my life. But of course, I just repeated that fanciful credits scene virtually every morning for seven years, and there was no 'inciting incident' that swept me up into an Oscar-nominated drama. Things that, when I tell the story of my life, sound like turning points, mostly happened little by little. Drama came through a drip-feed. I still had to unload the dishwasher. I still made typos. I still struggled to find matching socks.

In films, there's limited opportunity to run in circles: to have everything wound up in two hours, characters have to learn things fast. They quickly see the error of their ways and get back

67

on course. Heartbreak and failure are at best mild diversions, never catastrophes. Miscommunications are easily rectified; fall-outs never become rifts. And everything is so delightfully logical: if one relationship doesn't work out, it's because the protagonist was meant to be with the next guy she meets; if she gets fired, it's so she can pursue the dreams she has been pushing to the side-lines. Loss is always the gateway to something better. It might look like life can turn on a dime – will he get to the airport in time to tell her he really loves her? – but the movie gods make sure no one misses their true destiny and no potential goes unfulfilled. And, of course, they all live happily ever after. It all creates the illusion that once you've struggled through the challenge, that's it, job done, box ticked.

We often impose a similar narrative onto the events of history: the myth of progress. Having seen living conditions, life expectancy, and GDP rise over the twentieth century, many of us presumed that this was how things would be from now on: each generation would be healthier, wealthier and happier than the one which went before. Social mobility was surely inevitable. A rising tide was guaranteed to lift all boats. Alongside that, it was assumed that each scientific development and technological invention would leave us better off. Any suggestion of limiting our tinkering (because, for example, our inventions might be harming our mental health and relationships, enabling mass destruction, wreaking environmental destruction, or jeopardising livelihoods) would be to stand in the way of the new idol, Progress. To do so would have you branded a killjoy, a Luddite, a nostalgic fuddy-duddy.

By the early 1990s, we had seemingly come so far that Francis Fukuyama famously declared we had reached 'the end of history' as he believed liberal democracy and capitalism – which he saw as the endpoint of humanity's ideological evolution – were on the verge of being rolled out worldwide. There might still be 'events', but 'all of the really big questions had been settled' so 'in the post-historical period there will be neither art nor philosophy, just the perpetual caretaking of the museum of human history'. Economic calculation would govern everything; there would be no more need for things like imagination or poetry or courage.

It seemed believable for a while – the Berlin Wall had fallen; the Soviet Union was on the brink of collapse; and the market was booming. Five years later, Tony Blair's New Labour was swept into power to the tune of Things Can Only Get Better by (the aptly named) D:Ream. We had reached the third part of the drama: we would forever be living in our collective fairy tale ending.

And since this was the atmosphere which shaped how we saw the world, it comes naturally to many of us to presume the same will be true of our own lives. As we walk through a landscape of services and sales pitches all centred around our pleasure, it seems exceedingly normal to assume that we have a right to non-stop happiness. We imagine going from strength to strength, promotion to promotion, from dating to engagement to marriage to kids, from a 1-bed flat, to a 2-bed house and so on until we have spare rooms, studios, and studies that we wouldn't really know what to do with – except to fill with the stuff we never use. We can't really conceive of ageing or illness – these are, after all, the new taboos – and, anyway, the right anti-ageing cream will surely stop the hands of time. With our five-year plans mapped out, it is hard to fathom that we might find ourselves going 'backwards' without some speedy resolution and everything working out well for us after all.

But, as we know from having lived beyond the heady days of the nineties, things did not only get better, and western liberal democracy, Enlightenment-style rationality and the free market have not been embraced across the globe (and whether, if they were, that would represent the high point of humanity is a whole other question). We have seen a resurgence of religious fundamentalism, in the name of which, people are willing to commit horrific acts of violence; and we have seen the Far Right rise up to return the favour. Populism has reshaped the political landscape across Europe, and British society seems more ideologically divided than it has been in decades. And all the while the ticking clock of climate change continues in the background, bringing closer the very real possibility that we could make ourselves extinct by our love of consumption and convenience. Because, the most significant fly in the ointment is that perpetual progress is simply impossible: the environment does not have infinite resources to sustain a 'grow or die' mentality. And while some parts of society may reap the benefits of economic growth, others are pushed down or left behind.

Of course, classic feel-good films were meant to be vehicles for escapism, not accurate how-to guides to life. To leave us with the impression that the euphoria lasted forever, fairy tales and chick flicks cut away just at the moment the couple get together so that we don't see the arguments, the illnesses, the stresses of parenting, the grief of loss, or any of the other countless hurdles they are bound to encounter. Life just doesn't have that feeling of a satisfactory resolution, with all the loose ends being tied up, which films do.

There have been a few things that I thought would be my gateway to a happy ending. But, have you ever travelled somewhere exotic in the hope that somehow your 'emotional baggage' would not make it through customs and you'd find yourself utterly liberated and transformed, only to find that you took yourself with you – the whole kit and overthinking kaboodle? That's been me every time I crossed one of those finish lines. I'd expected to suddenly transform into a better version of myself, someone I could like and respect, someone I would be glad to introduce at parties. But when it comes to hoping external achievements and accolades will plug the gaps in shaky self-esteem, there's no such luck.

One of the first I'll-be-happy-whens I believed in was getting into Cambridge. 'If I go there, I'll be happy every day of my life', I remember saying when I was a teenager only to find that the Cambridge experience which existed in my head was vastly different to the one I would actually live and breathe, and the person I was in my daydreams was a total stranger to the 18-year-old who turned up with Ikea bags full of clothes, books and self-doubt. To make things worse, I even moved my own goalposts: to feel like I was enough, I figured I had to do more than just be enrolled there – I had to be one of the highest-performing students, be popular, and tot up enough impressive extra-curricular activities and internships for me to be employable straight after graduation. Unsurprisingly, that bar was impossibly high, leaving me with a whole pile of ammunition with which to shoot myself down if I ever felt an inkling of pride.

'I'll accept myself when I'm just a bit thinner', was another promise I made with myself over and over. But, even as the weight came off, that point of contentment proved to be a mirage, always just beyond the horizon, always demanding that I eat a bit less, and a bit less. And I only became more anxious, more withdrawn, and more fragile. The issue wasn't really my exam results or my figure: it was that, deep down, I didn't think I deserved to be happy. So, I would find ways of putting self-acceptance just a little further out of reach.

On top of these, there were milestones I thought I had to aim for on the grounds of social expectations and cultural norms. We are surrounded by visualisations of concepts like success, worth, love, sexuality and community because, rather than using factual descriptions of their products in their marketing, companies present fantasies of a dream existence, and suggest their products are a crucial part in that concoction. And even if we don't make a single purchase, we can still end up buying into these conceptualisations. In fact, given we see an estimated 5000 advertisements a day, it is hard to envisage these abstract ideas in terms that do not stem from the marketplace.

For women especially, finding Prince Charming is seen as an utterly essential ingredient in the recipe for happiness. Hence why so many items are sold as a means of winning over Mr Right. We have inherited the belief from eighteenth-century Romanticism that true love will put an end to any feelings of loneliness and alienation because the right partner will understand us completely, often without us having to utter a word of explanation. It's no wonder that we are looking to feel complete when our insecurities are constantly being probed open, deepened and multiplied. So, naturally, we search for some sort of proof that we are loveable. And, symptomatic of the sexism that still seeps through our society, it's the seal of approval from a man which is supposed to do the trick. Once we've got a diamond on our ring finger, we'll feel like we are enough.

It's easy to stumble into the trap of assuming that 'I will be happy when...' only to find that ups and downs, stresses and strains, disagreements and dreariness also characterise the land which we hoped would be full of greener grass. And even if our initial arrival on that verdant turf was as euphoric as we had hoped, the fluorescent feeling soon starts to fade. Thanks to a phenomenon called hedonic adaptation – a sort of diminishing return on happiness – we get used to the changes in our life which brought us floods of joy at first, and so those floods start to slow into a trickle and maybe, if we start to totally take them for granted, dry up completely.

Our once-new jobs, homes and romances become just the wallpaper to our daily to-do lists. The hundredth kiss doesn't give us the same rush as the first; there are irritating colleagues and stressful deadlines in the new office, just like the old; and the new house doesn't stay looking as glossy and pristine as it did in the estate agent's pictures. It isn't long before we need more happiness highs in order to feel satisfied. 'What is happiness?' asks the fictional advertising executive Don Draper in Mad Men. 'It's the moment before you need more happiness.'

Even if we do reach the end of the rainbow, success itself brings its own challenges. Make more money and you'll be more concerned about how your stocks and shares are faring, whether your bank might go under or taxes going up. Get married, and within a few years, you'll likely be worried about how to keep the romance alive while juggling children with a career and housework. Rise to the level of CEO and you'll have the fate of the whole company and all its employees in your hands. Become a household name and you'll soon have to defend your reputation and withstand intense scrutiny of your personal life. So we're prone to reset our metaphorical Sat Navs: same port of call, 'happiness', but this time via a different route. Those celebratory words 'You have arrived at your destination' are perpetually one horizon out of earshot.

Our belief in the possibility of attaining a 'happy ever after' could actually be the thing holding us back from deep contentment. Because even though, in our relatively privileged society, we are protected from so much of the hardship most of the world still bears, no life will ever, could ever, live up to the Disneyfied ideal. And supposing it could means that we are setting ourselves up for feelings of guilt, failure, bitterness, anger, or a poisonous brew of all of the above (depending on how you're wired) when our lives inevitably deviate from the yellow-brick road.

Research has shown, for example that those who believe in soulmates (i.e. that there is one person for whom you are destined) tend to be more anxious in relationships, less forgiving of their partner, and less committed to them when faced with difficulties – as any bump in the road is taken as evidence that this isn't 'the one' after all. The reality is that no one can understand (especially not intuitively) and adore every side of us, good, bad and ugly; a relationship cannot plaster over every hole in our character and extinguish all sense of vulnerability. After all, a partner will see you at your most emotional, your most irritating, and your most unrefined; they will see parts of you that none of your friends know about. So you are bound to, at times, feel exposed rather than pure ecstasy.

Nor can the feeling of butterflies endure forever. According to psychologists Elaine Hatfield and Richard Rapson, passionate love – that intense longing and attraction for your partner – lasts for a couple of years, and after this, 'companionate love' – a deep connection with and affection for the other – takes over. Joy can easily be found in both stages, but for those who solely associate the initial throws of passion with 'true love', this transition feels highly disturbing. They will likely be tempted to start to look for someone new who can get their heart racing, only to experience the same problem again later down the road.

And even though we all know the proverb 'money cannot buy happiness', that doesn't stop most of us trying to prove it to be false. Technically (although not quite as catchy a saying) earning up to around £60,000 a year *is* associated with higher levels of well-being and life satisfaction, but exceeding this threshold is detrimental to both of these scores. The more we strive to do so by, for instance, working longer hours or commuting greater distances to work, the less time we have for activities that are actually good for us, such as being with family and friends or in the great outdoors. Higher incomes also foster higher aspirations so that what we once considered extravagant is soon seen as a must. Travelling first class ceases to seem profligate – it becomes imperative; a wardrobe which once had a couple of designer items soon has to be filled with nothing else. And, if wealth opens a door to a slightly more well-to-do social circle, we are prone to still feel like the poor relative, no matter how much we have in the bank.

It might be material privilege and pampered lifestyles which get captioned #blessed on social media but, according to the New Testament, blessing has little to do with the trappings of wealth and status, and everything to do with God's presence with us. It is about sharing in the life of Jesus, the supremely blessed one, and thereby being redeemed, totally forgiven, blameless in God's sight, adopted as His sons and daughters, the apple of His eye. And it is also about being invited into a new family, a community that buckles all dividing walls, united under one Head and bound in love. And unlike the lap of luxury, this blessing isn't for a restricted elite: the God who is continually pouring Himself out in love between Father, Son and Holy Spirit, and out into creation cannot help but lavish this on all and sundry, irrespective of merit or prominence.

But to share in Jesus' resurrection life, we also have to share in His death, and so blessing demands sacrifice. To be 'blessed… among women', the Virgin Mary had to endure social stigma and gossip, risk abandonment by her betrothed, seek refuge in another country, and later watch her firstborn son executed as a criminal. 'A sword will pierce your own soul too', was *part of* Simeon's blessing to Mary as he prophesied over her new-born baby when she and Joseph went to present him at the Temple (Luke 2:35).

Blessing also has to, almost by its very nature, demand something of us because, as we have seen with the concept of hedonic adaptation, if we experience something unilaterally good without putting in any effort, we start to take it for granted. If moments of happiness were all I ever knew, I would not relish them; they would bore me. Contrary to what I might have expected, I have felt far closer to God at times when my prayers have just been ineloquent cries for help of 'I can't do this anymore', 'I don't know what to do, I'm so scared', or even just 'please' than when I have been delivering articulate speeches as prayers in public, with one eye on impressing the people with me.

And paradoxically, I have felt a strange sense of freedom when I have been forced to let go of things that I was clinging onto until my knuckles turned white. It has been as if my tiny self-oriented silo has broken open to give me a better glimpse of the world outside myself – its glory and its groaning – revealing what is truly significant beneath the smoke and mirrors. Joy has taken me by surprise, nestled in the darkest corners of my life, lurking even at rock bottom.

This isn't to say that times of pain, loss and suffering are actually good. No matter what you might have heard, God is not a sadist. But, love is at its most awe-inspiring when we feel it is undeserved. When we are at the end of ourselves, when it is no longer possible to pretend that we have all the answers, when we can no longer keep our walls up because we know we cannot make it on our own, then, and maybe only then, can we discover that God's love truly is unconditional.

And, if I am honest with myself, if anything has made me a more compassionate and courageous person, a better friend and less quick to judge, it has not been the times when I was riding a wave of privilege: it has been the battles which I thought would overwhelm me. The fruits of the Spirit in which we are called to grow rarely thrive on the greener grass we covet: we don't become more patient without being made to wait; we don't develop self-control without being sorely tempted. Maybe the way we learn to bless others, then, is always by having endured our own trials by fire first.

Because the point of blessing, whether it's spiritual strength and understanding or financial plenty, is for it to be shared out and passed on, especially to the least and the lost. God is always calling us to follow the example of His Son by using our advantage for the sake of others. When Abraham was blessed by God, and promised that he would become a great nation, God emphasised that this was 'so you shall be a blessing [...] And in you all the families of the earth will be blessed' (Genesis 12:3).

Let's put it this way: God cares more about the daily working conditions of those who make your clothes than the number of compliments you receive wearing them. He cares more about how the earth is creaking with the toxic waste produced by our obsession with gadgetry than He does about you getting the latest iPhone. So, if whatever it is that makes us feel favoured stokes our status and ego, but leaves anything else in God's creation worse off, then we need to wonder what or who we are really following.

Some churches, for example, boldly assert that health, wealth and happiness are yours to claim from God, as long as you have enough faith in God's ability to provide them, and ideally put your money where your mouth is by making a significant donation to the preacher as a 'thank you in advance'. Known as the prosperity gospel, this stream of theology presents the Bible as a contract between God and the believer and maintains that, because poverty and illness are part of the curse from which Jesus rescues us, they should form no part of the truly faithful Christian's life. If the individual is unshakeably certain that God can deliver whatever it is they want, then God will indeed supply it. No wonder, then, that this brand of Christianity is so popular – a religion built on a contract offers that oh so appealing sense of control. Clear terms and conditions, and the promise of a return on my investment? Sign me up.

Appealing, that is, until it appears that you do not have enough faith, no matter how hard you visualise and pray for that healing or that windfall which will help you make ends meet. Then you are left feeling more alone and guiltier than ever, because supposedly something you have or haven't done has prevented God from hearing your cry. Your frailty or sin was somehow so great that it disarmed the Almighty. In reality, such a treaty does not exist between God and His people, for God cannot be manipulated: 'the Lord your God is God of gods and Lord of lords, the great God, mighty and awesome, who shows no partiality nor takes a bribe', reads Deuteronomy 10:17. And since Jesus told us we cannot serve two masters, God and money, it seems clear that if we are using God as a means to a financial end, then the altar we are really worshipping at is that of materialism.

Even if we have avoided the worst of the scandals and abuses associated with the prosperity gospel (infamous for its pastors with multi-million-dollar homes and private jets, funded at the expense of their far less well-off congregants), our hyper-individualistic culture still frequently seeps into our religious practice. As someone who has a tendency to pray like I am reeling off a shopping list, I have too often misjudged the purpose of my faith to be that of any other consumer product or lifestyle choice: to make me feel good.

One of the most famous verses, plastered onto fridge magnets and coffee cups, which apparently proves that God has a happily-ever-after mapped out for us is Romans 8:28: 'We know that in all things God works for the good of those who love him, who have been called according to his purpose.' This is often taken to mean that everything happens for a reason, with an upgrade in our circumstances representing the end which God has in mind. God, in this telling, provides compensation for any hardship we experience, as if that suffering was a test for us to pass through to earn a prize at the end, or the result of God taking his eye off the ball and feeling bad about it. But grounding our faith in the goodness of God on the extent to which he meets our wish-list is a very risky business indeed because Romans 8:28 isn't addressed to us as individuals, and 'the good' which is being worked out isn't an improvement in our personal, material circumstances: it is a collective blessing, a promise to God's people as a whole.

The letter was written to a church under intense persecution by the Roman authorities – both Paul who wrote the letter and the church's members faced martyrdom for their faith. If their story had been penned by Hollywood producers, to whom senseless suffering is anathema, these early Christians would have been rescued just in the nick of time. Just as the first stone was picked up, the sword was lifted up, or the bonfire lit, God would send some dramatic rescue which would both save the believers and vindicate their cause. But the reality was far more brutal: the stones hit, the swords cut, and the fires crackled. In those instances, heaven seemed silent. 'My God, my God, why have you forsaken me?' even Jesus would cry aloud and receive no immediate answer (Matthew 27:46).

Any reading, then, of Romans 8:28 as a guarantee that God will protect us from harm and heartache runs foul of the fact that the letter's author and audience, the Old Testament prophets and God's own Son were not shielded from such suffering. When Paul wrote it, the Roman authorities seemed to be getting their way and annihilating this new community of Christians. So this part of the letter was supposed to reassure its readers that, no matter how bleak their future looked from the outside, God would use it to bolster the strength, faithfulness and mission of the whole Church.

Our individualistic culture also leads us to often misread a similar promise in the Old Testament: '"For I know the plans I have for you," declares the Lord, "plans to prosper you and not to harm you, plans to give you hope and a future"' (Jeremiah 29:11). God was speaking here through Jeremiah to the Israelites who had been exiled in Babylon. A false prophet, Hananiah, had announced that God was going to set Israel free within two years and Jeremiah was sent to pour proverbial cold water over this optimism. Just before the promise of 'plans to prosper' was uttered, Jeremiah told the Israelites they would be spending 70 years in captivity and that they should 'seek the peace and the prosperity of the city' in which they were exiles, for in its welfare they would find their welfare (Jeremiah 29:7).

That meant, contrary to what the Israelites surely wanted,

God was *not* going to wreak devastation on their enemies: God wanted to see Israel, His chosen people, bless the 'bad guy' Babylonians *before* the Israelites received their blessing from God – a reminder that God had only set Israel apart so that through them 'all nations on earth [would] be blessed' (Genesis 22:18). Because while we may consider anything that gives us a competitive advantage or sets us apart from the crowd to be a blessing, God is far less discriminating, causing the sun to rise on the unjust *and* the just (Matthew 5:45), the seed of the gospel to fall on the stony ground *and* the fertile soil (Matthew 13:1–23; Mark 4:1–20, and Luke 8:4–15), in the hope that all might come to know and love the ultimate Source of all flourishing, beauty and truth.

Given what we know about the events of the Babylonian exile, we know the 'you' for whom God had plans to prosper must have been the collective people of Israel rather than each one independently because, over that 70 years, thousands of individual Israelites would be brutalised and massacred, and only a tiny number would even live to see the promise of freedom and abundance fulfilled. The comfort of this much-quoted verse, then, was its reassurance that even when it looked like God had forgotten about Israel, God had not given up on them; although it seemed impossible for this ancient superpower to be knocked back, redemption would indeed come.

Hang on, a promise that applies to my children but not to me? One that doesn't prevent me from being hurt? One which requires patience, endurance and faithfulness even when it looks futile? I'm used to next-day delivery, instant gratification, and the whole world being accessible within a click, swipe or press. I think in terms of immediate results and quick fixes. But it turns out redemption cannot be ordered through my screen like a taxi or fast food, and God is not a wish-granting genie who will turn all my Pinterest inspiration into reality. This is hard to stomach for someone like me who suspects deep down that I am the centre of the universe.

Nevertheless, just because we in the West typically misread this verse by thinking it guarantees our personal comfort doesn't mean it is irrelevant to us. Christians are described as living as 'foreigners and exiles' (1 Peter 2:11) whose true 'citizenship is in heaven' (Philippians 3:20). So we, as a people, are not in a dissimilar condition to the Israelites living in Babylonian captivity, awaiting the rescue which we trust will come with Christ's return. Until then, we too have to be a blessing to those who curse us and, banking on God's constancy, live distinctively, in the other-centred way of love which Jesus modelled.

Our cultural obsession with living our best lives and squeezing as much in as we can – with bottomless bucket lists of things to do, places to see, books to read, and films to watch before you die – is connected to a declining belief in life after death. With heaven brushed aside as pie in the sky, 'opium for the masses' which keeps the oppressed classes content to go along with the status quo on earth, the burden on making the present utterly perfect is overwhelming. YOLO (you-only-live-once) and FOMO (fear-of-missing-out) go hand in hand: if you have only one life then you have to make every second count; you need to be sure you are having the most fun, the most success, the most happiness possible.

But as people confident of the resurrection, we know that the blessings we receive now are merely a foretaste of what is to come. The first Christians believed a happy-ever-after for the entire cosmos was imminent because they believed Jesus would soon return to judge the living and the dead. This radically relativised the value of everything they had previously built their lives around. They sold their possessions and property and shared the income among themselves, breaking down the distinction between the haves and the have-nots. They redefined the notion of family by opening their homes to anyone and everyone who wanted to follow the way of Christ. They were willing to sacrifice their own lives by caring for the sick, who had been outcast by Greco-Roman society.

They chose to live in the light of that approaching end, where love, justice and peace would reshape the whole world. But that end didn't come according to their anticipated timelines. And, under the influence of individualism and consumerism, many of us Christians are now half-hearted in our belief that Jesus might return in our own lifetimes, and so, like those around us, we focus on turning our own lives into a fairy tale instead.

Our desire for a happy-ever-after is, at root, about security, about feeling we cannot ever be attacked or experience loss again. But sadly, nothing in the world – not a self-help programme, not a special prayer, or all the money in the world – can make us immune from suffering. It took me a while to realise there wouldn't come a point when I could just coast through life: I might rise to some challenge, but there would just be different ones beyond it. I would continually need shepherding.

Jesus once told a story of a man who reached his 'happy ever after' and then expected to coast on his own success.

'Watch out! Be on your guard against all kinds of greed; life does not consist in an abundance of possessions.' And he told them this parable: The ground of a certain rich man yielded an abundant harvest. He thought to himself, 'What shall I do? I have no place to store my crops.' Then he said, 'This is what I'll do. I will tear down my barns and build bigger ones, and there I will store my surplus grain. And I'll say to myself, "You have plenty of grain laid up for many years. Take life easy; eat, drink and be merry."' But God said to him, 'You fool! This very night your life will be demanded from you. Then who will get what you have prepared for yourself?' This is how it will be with whoever stores up things for themselves but is not rich toward God. (Luke 12:15–21)

This rich man clearly felt #blessed: the harvest had turned out better than expected and given him enough to mean he'd never need to lift a finger again – provided he could find a way to keep the grain for his own use, and so he sets about building bigger barns. But God is pretty peeved to say the least, not because the farmer had done a good job and produced an abundant harvest, but because he had no intention of sharing his considerable surplus with those around him who were in need.

Jesus followed this parable with his famous teaching on anxiety, telling the crowds not to worry about what they will wear or eat, 'For the pagan world runs after all such things, and your Father knows that you need them. But seek His Kingdom, and these things will be given to you as well' (Luke 12:30–1). Look at the birds and the lilies, he gestured, they live day to day, but they do alright, don't they? They don't even have a concept of the future, so they can hardly make serious plans for it. Instead, they live moment by moment in reliance on God. And that is how it should be with us, Jesus suggests. Because no matter how much we feel like masters of the universe, the uncomfortable truth is, we aren't. We too are creatures in God's hands which, Jesus wants to remind us, are hands which cherish rather than withhold.

Jesus clearly understood how the pursuit of happiness and security often, paradoxically, breeds angst. As a matter of fact, research has shown the pressure to be happy tends to make us *more* anxious and afraid of failure. We try to pre-empt every possible risk, and make mitigation plans accordingly. We play out worst case scenarios in our head. We form strategies which are prone to reduce other people to pawns in our game of chess and overlook the ways in which God might move. In the process, we forget that God wants us to recognise our radical dependency on Him.

The man in the parable was, practically speaking, an atheist: he thought he had to provide for himself through carefully managing his own assets, with the almost inevitable result that he became miserly towards others. The same was true of the man who prompted Jesus to tell the story by asking 'Teacher, tell my brother to divide the inheritance with me': he was willing to rupture a relationship to protect his future material well-being.

The fact we are cared for by God doesn't mean we are indestructible: Jesus himself mentions that the flowers which God makes beautiful are 'here today and tomorrow thrown into the fire' (Matthew 6:30) and asks 'which one of you can by worrying add a single hour to your life?' (Matthew 6:27). So, this side of the new creation, mortality remains our lot. But despite the loss and suffering this entails, it can also provide a sense of relief. Because so much of our hustling comes from a place of trying to have God-like knowledge and control, as we assume that that could be the only way to feel safe and satisfied. Accepting your finitude and frailty, Jesus reminds us, isn't failure; it's freedom from an impossible imposition.

His teaching on this score is meant to bring our mind to the present, to remind us to slow down and breathe in God's goodness in our actual here-and-now life – not in the life we wish we had or in our life a couple more stations down the track. God's love is always, always enveloping you – as much now as in the past and as it will be in the future. Without reservations or regret.

One day, we will have the security and safety for which we yearn, and the truest desires of our heart, the ones set in us by God rather than those cultivated by a lifetime of advertisements, will be satisfied. That new Jerusalem is described as having no walls, because all threats and dangers will have been extinguished. Likewise, Revelation 21 says there will 'no longer be any sea' – the sea symbolising chaos – so we will no longer need to anticipate dangers and devise defence mechanisms. And, after millennia of tears, there will finally be no more death or mourning or crying or pain.

This is the finish line towards which all of creation is oriented. It may well lie beyond our individual life-spans, like it has for the millennia of Christians who have gone before us, and just like the fulfilment of many of the promises God made to the patriarchs (Abraham, for example, was told he would have as many progeny as there were stars in the sky, yet he died with only two sons; and Moses, whose mission was to bring the Israelites into the promised land, never got to enter it himself). But the fact that we are in good company when we walk in faith reminds us that this cosmic victory will flow not from our efforts but from the faithfulness of God. It is His purposes, not ours, which cannot be thwarted.

In the meantime, our duty is to this very moment – to live in the light of that coming Kingdom, to enact its ethic while we are in exile, and to prepare ourselves for perfect intimacy with God by daily shedding our concern with self-preservation and self-advancement, and being a channel for divine love and peace. We are to watch and wait, looking for the ways in which God is continually coming towards us, with our noses pressed to the glass in eagerness for that final coming when 'all shall be well, and all manner of thing shall be well', as Julian of Norwich put it.

So, given none of us can know what the future holds, I can't tell you what life has in store for you, as much as I wish, for both of us, that I could. I know that nothing will turn out as you expected. I know that there will be dark days as well as moments so beautiful that you barely dare blink. I know that your heart will ache with both sorrow and joy – and sometimes both at the same time. I know that love will open you up to grief that will make time stand still and your soul howl – and yet, I know that loving is what you are here for and that you will never regret those times that you loved until it ached. But most of all, I know that in all things and through all things, you will never be alone, never let go; that you are, and you will be, and you always have been, cherished beyond fathoming. And in those times when your soul is stilled within you, you will know that that is enough.

Circle Books

CHRISTIAN FAITH

Circle Books explores a wide range of disciplines within the field of Christian faith and practice. It also draws on personal testimony and new ways of finding and expressing God's presence in the world today.
If you have enjoyed this book, why not tell other readers by posting a review on your preferred book site.

Recent bestsellers from Circle Books are:

I Am With You (Paperback)
John Woolley

These words of divine encouragement were given to John Woolley in his work as a hospital chaplain, and have since inspired and uplifted tens of thousands, even changed their lives.

Paperback: 978-1-90381-699-8 ebook: 978-1-78099-485-7

God Calling
A. J. Russell

365 messages of encouragement channelled from Christ to two anonymous "Listeners".

Hardcover: 978-1-905047-42-0 ebook: 978-1-78099-486-4

Long Road to Heaven
The A Lent Course Based on the Film
Tim Heaton

This second Lent resource from the author of The Naturalist and the Christ explores Christian understandings of "salvation" in a five-part study based on the film The Way.

Paperback: 978-1-78279-274-1 ebook: 978-1-78279-273-4

Abide In My Love
More Divine Help for Today's Needs
John Woolley

The companion to I Am With You, Abide In My Love offers words of divine encouragement.

Paperback: 978-1-84694-276-1

From the Bottom of the Pond
The Forgotten Art of Experiencing God in the Depths of the Present Moment
Simon Small
From the Bottom of the Pond takes us into the depths of the present moment, to the only place where God can be found.
Paperback: 978-1-84694-066-8 ebook: 978-1-78099-207-5

God Is A Symbol Of Something True
Why You Don't Have to Choose Either a Literal Creator God or a Blind, Indifferent Universe
Jack Call
In this examination of modern spiritual dilemmas, Call offers the explanation that some of the most important elements of life are beyond our control: everything is fundamentally alright.
Paperback: 978-1-84694-244-0

The Scarlet Cord
Conversations With God's Chosen Women
Lindsay Hardin Freeman, Karen N. Canton
Voiceless wax figures no longer, twelve biblical women, outspoken, independent, faithful, selfless risk-takers, come to life in The Scarlet Cord.
Paperback: 978-1-84694-375-1

Will You Join in Our Crusade?
The Invitation of the Gospels Unlocked by the Inspiration of Les Miserables
Steve Mann
Les Miserables' narrative is entwined with Bible study in this book of 42 daily readings from the Gospels, perfect for Lent or anytime.
Paperback: 978-1-78279-384-7 ebook: 978-1-78279-383-0

A Quiet Mind
Uniting Body, Mind and Emotions in Christian Spirituality
Eva McIntyre
A practical guide to finding peace in the present moment that will
change your life, heal your wounds and bring you a quiet mind.
Paperback: 978-1-84694-507-6 ebook: 978-1-78099-005-7

Readers of ebooks can buy or view any of these bestsellers by
clicking on the live link in the title. Most titles are published in
paperback and as an ebook. Paperbacks are available in traditional
bookshops. Both print and ebook formats are available online.

Find more titles and sign up to our readers' newsletter at http://
www.johnhuntpublishing.com/christianity. Follow us on Facebook
at https://www.facebook.com/ChristianAlternative.